CW00868610

Hildebrand's Travel Guide

THAILAND BURMA

"This Sukhothai is a good place!
There are fish in the waters, rice grows in the fields.
The King does not tax his subjects...
The faces of the people are happy."

(An inscription in stone found at the remains of the former royal city of Sukhothai, between 1238 and 1349, capital of the first Thai kingdom in Siam).

Publisher
K+G, KARTO+GRAFIK Verlagsgesellschaft mbH
© All rights reserved by
K+G, KARTO+GRAFIK Verlagsgesellschaft mbH
Schönberger Weg 15–17
6000 Frankfurt/Main 90
First Edition 1985
Second Edition 1988
Printed in West Germany
ISBN 3-88989-076-8

Distributed in the United Kingdom by
Harrap Columbus,
19-23 Ludgate Hill,
London EC4M 7PD
Tel: 01 248 6444

Distributed in the United States by
HUNTER Publishing Inc.,
300 Raritan Center Parkway,
Edison, New Jersey 08818
Tel: 201 225 1900

Author
Dr. Dieter Rumpf

Photo Credits
C. J. Eicke,
Ingrid Hagen, Monika Henseling,
Dr. Dieter Rumpf, Klaus Wolff,
Bernd Limbart, Sallwey

Illustrations
Eckart Müller, Peter Rank, Manfed Rup

Maps
K+G, KARTO+GRAFIK Verlagsgesellschaft mbH

Translation
Margaret Heberer

Lithography
Haußmann-Repro, 6100 Darmstadt

Type Setting
LibroSatz, 6239 Kriftel

Printed by
Schwab Offset KG, 6452 Hainburg/Hess.

Hildebrand's Travel Guide

Impressions
Photographs p. 6
Travel Experiences and Reflections p. 48

Information
Land and People p. 70
Your Travel Destination from A to Z p. 166
Useful Information p. 185
Contents p. 190

Supplement: Travel Map

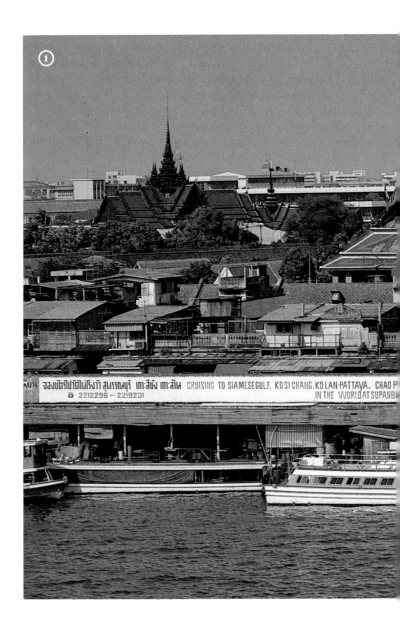

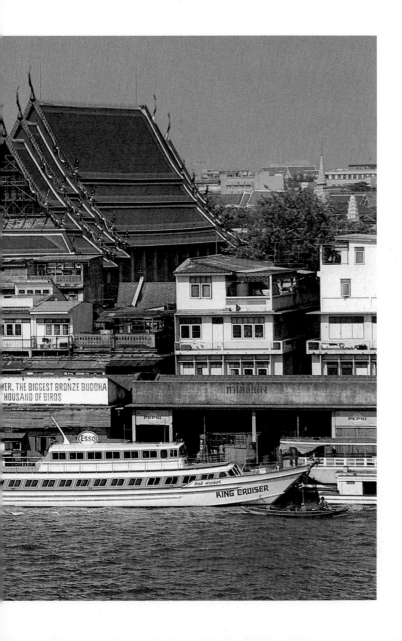

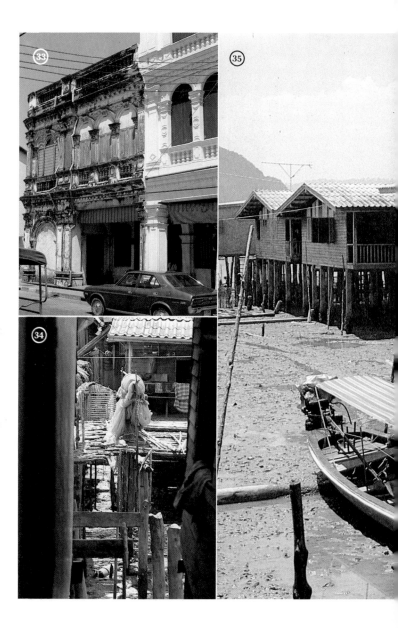

Captions

1. The lifegiving Chao Phaya (Menam) separates Bangkok from Thonburi and supplies water for the rice baskets of Central Thailand.

2. Three-wheeled taxis, cheap and a major means of transport.

3. This picture is not exactly typical of Thailand's railway. Air conditioned carriages and sleeping cars are available on main routes of the fairly well developed system.

4. Bicycle rickshaws are found in many towns and villages of any size. Korat in particular is famed for the number of this cheap means of transportation.

5. Working elephants are the tractors of the jungle. Once a year, in November, the pachyderms can be seen at the elephant round-up at Surin in east Thailand (see under "In a Jumbo, to see the Jumbos").

6. A significant economic factor and colourful too: the floating markets of Burma and Thailand. Very photogenic is the market at the Burmese Inle Lake and in Thailand in Bangkok and Damnoen Saduak – around 100 km south of Bangkok.

7. The pulse of the Burmese economy is what's offered at the open-air markets, held every day in larger towns.

8. Young "Sons of Buddha": almost every faithful Thai and Burmese turns his/her back on the world for at least a few weeks and retreats to a monastery.

9. A market-woman carried her wares in a fashion typical for Southeast Asia.

10. Thais start at a young age training for cock-fights. Cock-fighting, widespread in Southeast Asia, is possibly based on ancient blood rites.

11. Street stalls – snack bars Bangkok style. Generous portions and cheap, good too; strongly recommended for tourists as well.

12. Imaginative wares on sale at Thailand's potteries.

13. Puppet shows played a significant role in the development of Burmese culture. A marionette hung on up to 60 strings and there was even a Minister for this art (see under: "Marionettes Hang on 60 strings – and Dance").

14. Chiang Mai in Thailand's north is not only famous for its pleasant climate and beautiful temples; colourful, imaginatively painted parasols are also sold here.

15. Girls performing traditional khon dances in Bangkok. Connoisseurs have called this court dancing of the Thai living classism. In bygone days the dancers had to be sewn into their costumes. A state financed institution and tourists keep this ancient art alive.

16. In festive dress young Thai girls pay tribute at the temple.

17. Woodcarving is a highly developed skill in Burma and Thailand and once more Chiang Mai is a major centre.

18. The same applies to silver work, and the craftsman needs only the simplest tools for the most intricate designs.

19.–25. Peoples of many races – in addition to Thai there are so-called minorities which make up around 10% of total population; Karen, Akha, Yao, Meo or Lahu and Lisu stem for the most part from the south of China, and have until now not been assimilated into Thai culture, but still pursue their traditional way of life.

26. Rice – still the major agricultural product of both countries. Earlier export volume was much greater but there has been a marked drop in recent years. Burma however still covers 60% of all exports with rice.

27. Winning salt in Thailand, an interesting subject for photographs.

28. Sun, sea and sand – Thailand's beaches, above all on the Gulf of Siam attract sun-worshippers from all parts of the world. Hardly less beautiful, but less well known, or inaccessible, the Burmese beaches. The beach at Ngapali in the Burmese Arakan State (near Sandoway) is the "hot tip" among those in the know.

29. Bathing paradise with bizarre cliff formations to be found chiefly in the south of southern Thailand (among others Phangna).

30.–32. Splendid tropical vegetation thanks to adequate rainfall and even temperatures. Whether giant Baobab trees (30) yellow-flowering acacias (31) or bushes such as bougainvillea – Thailand and Burma are blessed with a vast variety of flora.

33.–35. House types: fishermen's houses on piles at the tidal coasts (35) town houses bearing the imprint of Asiatic colonial times (33) or city slum areas housing the influx of people from the rural areas.

36. Ascent to the temple on Doi Suthep, the loveliest pagoda in north Thailand. Mythological snakes (nagas) serve as balustrades.

37. Soaring heavenwards: Thai-Chedi, which – with local differences – are found throughout the country.

38. Ananda Temple is considered a perfect example of Mon-Burmese architecture, at Pagan (see under: "The Name of Perfection ist Ananda").

39. Twilight on Shwe Dagon Pagoda, Rangoon; small pagodas crowd round the mighty main Stupa; Shwe Dagon is praised as the most impressive sacral structure of Southeast Asia (see under "Gold in the City").

40. Temple architecture of the Thai; Chedi (left), Mondhop (centre) and Prang (at right behind) in one picture.

41.–43. Decorative feature on Thai temples: Cho-fah (41) the history behind this decoration can no longer be determined precisely, depiction of Garuda (42) and heavenly beings. Garuda pack animal of the Indian god Vishnu is also the heraldic animal of Thailand. His origin: he is considered the sun eagle of the Aryan peoples.

44. Thailand's art and culture reached their peaks at Sukhothai and later Ayutthaya. Even today the large statues of Buddha in ruined and decaying temples are decorated with holy flags and almost daily tribute is paid with flowers, paper flowers or fruit.

45. In Wat Si Chum of Sukhothai is the 14 metre (46 ft) high statue of Buddha which is surrounded by a three metre thick wall with secret passage. From an opening behind the head, the king fired his generals on in battle as the "Voice of Buddha".

46. Buddhas perfect to the last detail also in Burma. This standing Buddha is in a side temple at Shwezigon Pagoda in Pagan and represents the classic Mandalay Period, last of the Burmese styles.

47./48. Reclining Buddhas, mainly as monumental figures are seen frequently in Burma and Thailand. This position does not however always depict Buddha's entry into Nirvana, the highest aim of Buddhism, sometimes these also depicting the "Resting Buddha".

49. Following the teachings of enlightenment – Thai monks meditating.

50. In the east of Thailand, such as displayed on this Buddha from Phimai near Korat, Cambodian Khmer influence are evident.

51. Typical head of a Thai Budda; Thai art reached its peak first during the Sukhothai Period and later in the Ayutthaya Period.

52. Stone surrounds and door leaves at many Thai temples and monasteries are artistically worked. In many cases the teak doors are also decorated with enamel work or mother-of-pearl.

53. Asiatic and European influences meet chiefly at the Grand Palace; here the entrance gate to the Audience Hall.

54. These Thai ghost houses are considered living quarters for the spirits (see under "Phi and Nat – A Ghost House"). There are regular factories producing these small houses and they are set up, among other places, also at dangerous road junctions as a protection against accidents.

55. Inthas the famous leg rudderers of the Burmese Inle Lake. This people came originally from the area around Tavoy and migrated to the Inle Lake.

56. Rice is threshed in the traditional manner in the fields.

57. Festively dressed Inthas under white ceremonial umbrellas on a ceremonial ship of the Inle Lake. These barges are used during the famous Karaweik Festival.

58. Bamboo is split, wet and then woven into mats; in this way whole walls of houses are made.

59. Ceremonial barges on Inle Lake in the Shan State of Burma; once a year during the Karaweik Festival four small effigies of Buddha are transported to villages in, and on, the lake – as bestowers of blessings.

Gold in the City

Rangoon, capital of Burma since 1886, has seen better days. The streets around the wharves on the Rangoon River, which flows into the sea 30 kilometres (18.6 miles) away, must have jostled with life. In every sense of the word. Bars, dives, doss houses, one after the other, something for everyone; and right next door, the "Strand Hotel" with rooms floored in solid teak for those demanding better things.

And the "Strand" too, as it's fondly referred to by elderly globetrotters with a faraway gleam in their eyes, has also seen better days. Adventurers describing tiger hunts in glowing terms, dubious businessmen seeking their luck (and seldom finding it!) in trading, seamen from all corners of the world and artists who wove the fabric of dreams and visions from the exotic surroundings – they all exchanged experiences and memories at the hotel bar. Tips on the "specialties" offered in the riverside dives were exchanged among insiders "under the counter", in a manner of speaking. Rangoon, it must have been something like Eldorado around 50 years ago, and even in 1920 it was still the biggest rice port in the world.

The facade is crumbling. And not only from the houses in an architectural style reminiscent of bygone colonial days, which doesn't by any stretch of the imagination mean that the city, with 2 million inhabitants, has become dull and colourless. It will always remain colourful, no matter what. This is certain, not only because of the noisy, ramshackle traffic, or the exotic flowers and shrubs in the small gardens, but also because of the people themselves in their ancient national dress, the longyi, a sarong draped casually around the hips which seems to defy all the laws of gravity.

More than anything else however it is the Buddhistic temples, and one in particular, that dominate a Rangoon – shuttered and locked-up by 9 p.m. at latest, which has become so straitlaced – soaring and gleaming, they range into the blue skies. There is gold in the city.

After the markets and harbour, they form the high spots of every sight-seeing tour. The Sule Pagoda at the heart of the city, right next door to the offices of the national tourist board "Tourist Burma", is said to be the oldest, some 2,500 years; Botataung, alongside the harbour, is almost as venerable, octagonal with inner courts, something rarely found in Burma. Kaba Aye on the other hand, the pagoda of "World Peace" was only built around 30 years ago for the sixth Buddhistic Council.

The crowning glory – in every sense – is the Shwe Dagon Pagoda, the "Golden". It can quite simply be described as the city's landmark. Rangoon without Shwe Dagon would be like music without melody. More than one visit is really a must; during the day, at twilight and in the cool dark of evening.

This most impressive of Burmese pagodas was given its name before Rangoon existed. Later to become, in its majestic beauty, the most revered of all Buddhistic shrines, at first it was nothing more that the pagoda of the fishing village Dagon. But even then the main stupa was gilded (shwe = gold). When in the middle of the 18th century the Burmese king, Alaungpaya, ended his campaign, he changed the name Dagon to Yangun (= end of war), which later became Rangoon. And the Shwe Dagon gained more and more in

Burma – Birma
Burmese – Birman

German speakers often make life difficult for themselves with their language, just a glimpse in the pages of that bible of the German language, Duden, pinpoints this, and this regrettably also applies to Burma, Burmese or Birmans. Or should we say Birma? The French call the country Birmanie, the Russians say Birma, Italiens – Birmania; English speakers pronounce it Barma – picked up from the Indians, their onetime colonial subjects. In keeping with the confusion of pronunciations it is written here as "Burma". And we have adopted this – and are entirely wrong: Birma would be right.

There are similar problems with the inhabitants: Burmese describes all the people living here, and Birmans too. They would however most likely protest at being lumped together under one term – in the same way as the Scots, Irish and Welsh protest against "English" being used for all natives of the United Kingdom – and counter with Karen, Shan, Mon, Kachin. Confusing?

It was mainly the Portuguese, and to some extent Italians, who, in the 15th and 16th centuries, brought the term "Birma" to Europe. These seafarers made the first contact with the Mon living in the south of the country. These however called the area much further to the north, settled by Birmans, "Mbirma". The tongue twisting "M" was soon dropped in Europe. And an error persists: in this book the land is called "Burma", following the dictates of everyday language. Burmese is used to describe all the inhabitants, whilst Birman indicates that dominant group of today, who settled last in the country and established the great kingdom of Pagan.

The Burmese themselves, by the way, call their country "Maynma", the Shans say "Man" and the word "Bama" has become rooted in colloquial language.

---

splendour. Today the main stupa soars 107 metres (351 ft) into the heavens.

Condensed history: Shwe Dagon was first mentioned in annals of 1362 when the Mon king, Binnya U, increased its height to 60 feet: 400 years later the pagoda reached its present height under King Ssinnbiuschin and he, in the same manner as rulers before him, commanded that he be weighed in gold, with the exception that the gold was to be used to plate the main stupa.

It would seem however that this is not exactly how events took place. Even today Thailanders look askance towards the west in the direction of Rangoon and Shwe Dagon, apparently not without reason, for rumour has it, that the pagoda's gold was plundered from Ayutthaya by the Burmese during the sack of that former Thai capital. Compulsory building scheme: Ayutthaya went up in flames in 1767 after a two year siege...

Special care was devoted to the hti, the umbrella which crowns the stupa. Hundredweights of pure gold were further embellished with innumerable precious stones.

The Burmese themselves regard the history of their pagoda less soberly.

A legend, such as could only be told in Asia, graphically describes the creation of this splendid sacred monument. The Burmese myth surrounding the Singuttara mound where Shwe Dagon was built, starts with a scorpion which devoured elephants and continues with two brothers who, 2,400 years ago, brought eight hairs from the holy beard of Buddha to just this place where the pagoda stands today; lightning flashed, the earth trembled, a beam of light crept out of a deep pit – the sacred place for the relic was found. Led by Sakkra, God of gods, mediator between Heaven and Earth, all the gods and spirits, escorted by seductive, heavenly, dancing girls (apsaras), filled the pit with jewels. And in memory of all these wondrous things the people crowned the sacred place with a solid gold stupa.

It is more than likely that even in pre-buddhistic times the Singuttara mound was the site of first an animistic, and then Hindu, shrine.

In the soft light of the evening sun three young women kneel before a small Buddha, next to one of the 64 smaller stupas, which are grouped around the main building. An old man pours holy water over the figure in a purification ceremony: with lotus blossoms in their hands, the three bow to the ground three times, once for Buddha, once for his teachings and once more for the monks. Then they place their flower offerings on the small altar, bow again in the same way, tighten the longyi around their hips, and start on their devotional circuit of the stupa – in a clockwise direction.

The three women had come up via the south stairway which leads, guarded by a pair of grim faced lions (Leogryphs) more than 10 m (33 ft) high,

from the foot of the hill to the uppermost platform. The most important of the four stairways for the quarters of the heavens, and the one most frequently used. For anyone looking for an easier way of ascent, there is an ugly, but fully functional, lift for tired visitors. But then the picturesque devotional shops are missed. Numerous halls for meditation and rest (tassaung) flank the marble paved walk. Opposite them, the 64 smaller stupas which crowd round the main pagoda like timid children. These are said to be the result of private donations. And everywhere, Buddhas.

A triumph of ingenuity: a special place of honour, close to the western approach, is occupied by the 16 ton bell, Mahaghanta, which was cast in the 18th century. The Burmese are very proud that it still stands here today; and rightly so, it would seem, for during the second Anglo-Burmese war in 1852, the British are said to have loaded the bell on a ship bound for Calcutta, a venture which ended in the heavy treasure falling into the muddy waters of the Irrawaddy Delta, where it resisted all salvage efforts.

Then the Burmese offered their assistance, but subject to the condition that the bell stayed in the country. Divers pushed hundreds of thick bamboo staves into the mud under the bell, it is related that some 1,000 men heaved as one, the bell rose to the surface and into Burmese care once more. Since that time the bell is holier than ever before.

A tip for photographers: the best picture postcard view of Shwe Dagon is taken from the north stairs. But before that one or two things might appear curious to visitors to Burma. In one hall, flanked by two dancing guards –

where the faithful do homage to the footprint of Buddha – pilgrims can be seen wetting ears and nose. The reason? The water is considered holy with miraculous powers which give protection against diseases of the eyes and ears. Prophylaxis Burmese style.

But the most vivid and moving impression one takes away from Shwe Dagon is that of living faith surrounding this splendid structure, which in spite of size and sheer massiveness, so clearly demonstrates the spiritual quality of late Burman sacral architecture. Anyone taking the time to watch – from some quiet corner – for one or two hours, the activities around the stupa, probably learns more about Buddhism and Burma, than others in too much of a hurry with far too many other pagodas on their itineraries.

Rangoon would indeed be poorer without Shwe Dagon, but instead it is still a city which sparkles, merely having shed the cheap glitter. An evening at the Karaweik Restaurant, a copy of a Chinese barque or one of the ceremonial barges of the Inle Lake (named after a mythological bird) accompanied by Burmese music and dance, emphasizes this: unpretentious, relatively authentic and very, very, impressive.

No Olives in the Village

Bangkok – that is for me the gateway to the beauties of tropical Asia: and – without warning – plunges me into all the ugliness and evidence of faulty development to be found on this continent. Contradictory impressions which aren't wiped out but rather provoked by Bangkok. A city which is more than that – Bangkok is a condition.

The "City of Angels" (Krung Thep) catapulted around 200 years ago from an insignificant market place on the east bank of the Chao Phaya (= Menam), called Olive Village, and became capital of the still reigning Thai dynasty. Victorious Burmese troops had so thoroughly destroyed the previous capital Ayutthaya that no attempt was made towards restoration. The Thai commanding general, Taksin, got away by the skin of his teeth, gathered the remains of his troops and turned to Thonburi, today a "suburb" of Bangkok, on the other bank of the Menam. Mad dreams of power led to his downfall out of which there arose the Chakri Dynasty (1782). Rama I crossed the river, and the monstrous growth of Bangkok had begun.

It's no easy matter to come to terms with this city in any sense. She is like a drug where you don't know if the experience is going to be pleasant or something you are going to deeply regret.

What goes on in the heads of those who arrive here for the first time? The drive from Don Muang Airport to the centreless city alone makes the value of our highway regulations abundantly clear. Absolute chaos. Everyone drives according to his own rules, and so not only the heat and smell would bring the sweat to the brows of even our most hardened asphalt cowboys.

Then there is the sheer mass of humanity. More than 10% of the total population of Thailand lives here, around 5 million souls. No one has ever really bothered to count. Home for many is the street.

But in spite of the traffic turmoil, in spite of noise, exhaust fumes and ⟶ throngs of people in streets lined with buildings which look as if the architects had competed in dreariness – this city grips and stirs the imagination. What has long become routine in other places, is met again in Bangkok as if for the first time. Contradictions over and over again.

Prasat

Stressed tourist faces in the hotels. Stress seems to be the very stuff of life, not only for the natives. I was curious enough to make something like an unrepresentative poll: Would you ever come back to Bangkok? Almost every single stress victim answered with an unhesitating "Yes".

A typical sightseeing tour looks something like this: first the ugly Wat Trimitr with its famous Golden Buddha, which was found by chance. Then of course, shirt sleeves rolled down, and a ban on shorts – past the guards to the Grand Palace in all its neoclassicist inelegant, awkwardness; it couldn't be more wooden. Thank heaven that in the neighbouring Wat Phra Keo, the royal temple, traditional Thai culture asserts itself once more. A quick glance around, often in the crush of other rubber neckers, at the so-called Emerald Buddha, which is really made of nephrite or greenstone, and can only be seen really clearly by the most eagle eyed, positioned as it is under the temple roof.

Then on once more in the wild traffic chase, besieged on all sides by souvenir hawkers when getting in and out of the bus, to the museum, which really is worth seeing. The hothouse climate however ensures that by the Marble Temple (Wat Benchamapopitr), at the latest, even the most determined tourist runs out of air. But the itinerary still hasn't been completed. Wat Po, with massage in the temple, and Wat Arun in Thonburi on the west bank of the Menam are musts in every tour programme, which could go even further. Immediately beyond the walls of the temple where monks meditate in saffron yellow robes, roaring city traffic.

If your main interest is culture you must be completely satiated by now. The elegance and, almost casual, beauty of Thai temples, once dismissed as Bangkok wedding cake style, leave an impression: artistic intensity of the late period paired with deep faith can hardly be seen or experienced in such abundance anywhere else.

Bangkok however polishes its tourist image with another persuasive pleasure: shopping! If anyone looking for almost anything at all, can't find it here then they didn't look hard enough, or whatever was being looked for couldn't have been had any other place either.

The shops around the top hotels and along the shopping malls are fully capable of making even the most careful penny pincher develop Croesuslike ambitions.

Ranging from valuable Thai silks in beautiful colours and tasteful designs, to selected and expensive antiques, from all kinds of handicrafts to wonderful wood carvings, from Kitsch to high art – everything is on offer. Parasols sell just as well as examples of the silversmith's work or ivory carvings, and certificates are handed out testifying to the authenticity of jewels, gold and similar tempting trinkets. Who could fly home empty handed?

Apart from temples, nothing, the culture fan could express the impression gained: shopping ranging from good to excellent could be that of the consumer: girls at every corner that of the night hawks. It would take more than a pinch of masochism to judge everything favourably. In spite of all – Bangkok still stirs the imagination, again and again.

Prabat paints big posters in glaring colours aimed at tempting cinema goers into seeing the latest tear jerker churned out at the antlike studios of Bombay. He has a family and was born in Bangkok. Happy as he is to drive off in his small car "Made in Japan" to the coast at week-ends, he is just as happy

to get back again. "Take Bangkok the way it is. Noisy, hot, sticky and ugly. A marvellous town!".

Who can contradict him? For my friend Prabat goes to the temple in the evening, lights the joss sticks and pays tribute to the wisdom of the teachings of Buddha. These teach him that nothing is forever. And when he sees the crowded ships on the city's canals, the few remaining Khlongs, in the soft evening light, when he sweating, swearing, with his hand on the horn, fights his way through the chaos of the Silom Road – what is today measured in time? What does today count in the scheme of things?

Passage of the present, flowing into the future – seems to be the key to understanding this city.

Simple tools for artistic metal work.

Each time I leave Bangkok I'm happy to get away. And then an inexplicable feeling, something between sadness and longing. Something I can't describe. Bangkok.

Pattaya – Romance à la carte

The picture is always the same. Hotel, bus, tourists all interchangeable: there we sit, around 20 of us in a bus parked in front of a luxury hotel waiting to drive off: the air conditioning works quietly, but efficiently. Hothouse atmosphere in refrigerator temperatures, shivering we look forward to the sunfilled days in front of us. Sun, shining white beaches, blue seas, waving palm trees and a restaurant picturesquely perched close to the sea. A Dream, to become reality at Pattaya.

The road to the Eastern Gulf of Thailand is surprisingly good. Pattaya is about 140 kilometres (89 miles) away and the bus will take about two hours for the trip. Outside, flat, contourless contryside passes by giving hardly time for more than a fleeting glance, seemingly only given some sort of structure with road signs like Chonburi or Bang Saen, and making our wish to get there stronger with each mile: Pattaya, Thailand's favourite Fata Morgana, begins to materialise.

Disappointment then when we finally arrive. Right at the outskirts of the town, a housing estate shows the rotten teeth of misguided town planning: gray concrete thrown up without feeling or imagination, already displaying the first signs of decay before completion: dusty, empty, pavements under the hot midday sun. Even the sign advertising "very good massage" which seems to promise a lot, and no doubt keeps its word, fails to wipe out the dreariness. Suddenly I remember "High Noon" with the show down, that deadly duel at the end. I feel just as abandoned as the hero, just as disillusioned. Was I expecting too much of Pattaya?

Then a sigh of relief as the bus turns right away from the Sukhumvit Highway in the direction of Pattaya Beach. Here now spread out before us lies what we were searching for; the blue waters of the gulf, white beaches and – even if blowing somewhat wildly in the wind – palms as a flattering contrast. Nature which has been so extravagant here had survived, more, had asserted itself. Flowers and shrubs soften the lines of the new buildings lining the beach road (excuse me; but promenade would be just a slight exaggeration).

Wild building schemes and speculators have – in spite of some determined efforts – been unable to disfigure the face of Pattaya. At least not till now. Before the Vietnam war everything was very different here. A few fishermen's huts of straw and bamboo, colourfully painted boats rocking in the dunes, sunbrowned children overflowing with life on the beach, velvety nights which can be so yearningly, melancholy here. All these belong to the past, changed by the arrival of the GIs. These men were more than just glad to escape the murderous jungles of Vietnam if even only for a few weeks, and looked for more than recreation and dolce farniente on the enchanting beach ever alternating with the waves.

Hotels rose accompanied by restaurants, night clubs and bars; fishermen changed their nets for trays and became waiters or hawkers, taxi drivers and hotel staff; ruthless leisure industry managers drilled the sleepy village into becoming a mondane beach resort: girls all over Thailand climbed into long distance buses to try their luck at the new Eldorado. Pattaya wasn't exactly kissed awake like the Sleeping Beauty, but it wasn't able to doze any longer either.

Then after the soldiers left, linked to Bangkok by a good road, the Sleeping Beauty tempted foreign tourists with an enticing smile. They came, and still come, with pleasure and willingly. With dreams in their eyes. It's perfectly clear that innocence has sufferd all down the line, but the Thai Sleeping Beauty has for all that not become ugly and tired.

Sun, sea, idyll à la Robinson. Sport and high life with lots of glamour are the baits put out enthusiastically by shrewd professionals to tempt the world weary. And they are not entirely wrong. But something became clear to me as I strolled along the main street in south Pattaya. Here where the action is, where the outsiders have dug in, Thailand has lost that special Thai something. "Berlin" and "Hank's Hideaway", "Mario's" and "Bonanza Court", "Hofbräu" and "Le Jean Bart", signalise that internationality which loves to bathe in jet set limelight, and only gets a sunburn for its pains.

For Pattaya has remained, what it always was, a village. A lively village, true, in which the first cock crow often enough gets lost in the hustle, bustle and gaiety; perhaps vital too, able to take many a downward trend in the graph of tourist popularity; certainly not a pretty village, since too much took place too quickly without any real planning, but always exciting and stimulating from every point of view.

Particularly exciting; a glimpse into the waters. The twin islands of Koh Larn and Kooh Sak, off the coast of Pattaya draw even Thai diving clubs; a wonderland of colour and shape at depths of between 7 to 15 metres (23 to 49 ft); bizarre corals, fish of every size – from gray to billposter coloured – Pattaya is at its most beautiful underwater, even just snorkelling makes this very clear. The days don't fly, they float away in the indescribable symphony of colours in this silent world at the bottom of the sea.

I wanted to explore this underwater fairyland even more thoroughly. The Thai diving instructor managed to turn a complete ignoramus into a promising pupil in just one week, able to handle mouthpiece and airbottles as if to the manner born. And groups of four get a discount at Pattaya's diving schools where techniques of deep sea diving are made to seem almost child's play.

And then the moment of truth; the first real diving session off the south tongue of Koh Larn. An explosion of colours and shapes in this giant aquarium, into which you glide apparantly weightlessly. But even 10 to 15 metres (33 to 49 ft) down you don't remain alone for long; others too have fallen victim to the magic of the underwater world. They come from the hotels at Nuan Beach on Koh Larn where a new leisure centre, including golf course, is developing.

It's quieter in the waters around Koh Sak (7 to 10 metres / 23 to 33 ft), Koh Lin and Ko Pai, where the bottom drops down to 25 metres (82 ft) and one is almost alone with the fish, corals and shells. A silent intercourse, which is better limited to speaking with your eyes, touching is risky and can lead to painful injuries. The islets of Koh Pai and Koh Lin can be reached in one hour by boat from Koh Larn.

It was during diving, at the very latest, that I realised I had fallen completely in love with the coast and islands of the Gulf of Thailand.

Love is something which abounds in Pattaya. For those who can, free, for those who can't, and that's most, hard cash. Haadyai, Bangkok and Pattaya – heady names in a heady climate. The completely unabashed "you like girl, sir?" touted by Tom, Dick and Harry for the tourist's pleasure, still rings in my ears. Girls who at an early age follow one of the oldest professions in the world and take pleasure in turning night into day. The bars are really lively, not everyone's taste, but it's just as certain that not many will complain.

Holidays, vacation, and lazing – Pattaya is ideal. Recipe for doing nothing; get up late and greet the no longer dew fresh, day with an opulent breakfast at the hotel pool side; cold drinks and hot food imbibed in the cool shadows out of the tropical sun; then just dawdling around, maybe shopping (South Pattaya), an ice here, a king size prawn there; more than likely with a thoroughly upset stomach, enjoy the evening on the terrace of some restaurant overlooking the sea and watch the sun sink into the ocean like a ripe orange. Bliss! Let yourself be lulled by the rapidly gathering night... days can drift past like this in Pattaya, too.

All those left cold by dolce farniente in the hot sun, must at least be a gourmet. All kinds of seafood take pride of place on the menus, but not cheap. Tourism has led to spiralling prices.

A watery salto mortale in a borrowed boat because a daring attempt was made to cope with waves that were greater than the skills of the intrepid skier; hanging on the end of a rope being towed like a kite by a boat for – a bird's eye view of Pattaya, on water skis over the bumpy waters of the gulf or just plain swimming – sporting opporunities for the active are almost unlimited. Golf and walking, going out to sea with the local fishermen or watching trained elephants, cock fights or traditional dances at Nong Nooch Village, only 15 kilometres (9.3 miles) south of Pattaya – everything is possible.

Certainly Sleeping Beauty has turned into a rather thorny rose; a fishing village has become a stronghold of the leisure industry with lots of light, and a shadow side too. Pessimists forecast the worst; the whole gulf from Sattahip to the Cambodian border will be blown up into a sort of gigantic leisure monster in which Hovercraft rip shrill furrows in the, at present, quiet waters.

Whether this will ever come about is still written in the bright stars in the night sky over Pattaya.

Rudder Legs

You've read right, not rubber, rudder. The waters of Inle Lake, some 22 kilometres (13.7 miles) long and 11 (6.8 miles) wide, lie like a mirror before us; glittering in the strong rays of the morning sun, a chain of mountains 1,700 metres (5,577 ft) high shelters this largest lake in Upper Burma from the Yaunghwe District in the south

Shan states: the morning mist has dyed them blue.

Our group of 14 had just arrived from Taunggyi, where we had spent the night at the romantic "Raunggyi Strand", at Yaunghwe, a village on the lake. During the bus trip over the serpentine roads from the plateau on which Taunggyi, the Shan capital, lies down into the valley of the lake, our hobby photographers had certainly got their money's worth. The one hour trip is well worthwhile in spite of bumpy tarred roads. A boat trip on Inle Lake is just as much a must in every tourist round trip itinerary as Shwe Dagon in Rangoon, the enormous pagoda complex in Pagan and sightseeing in the last Burmese royal capital, Mandalay. For those who can arrange it, the boat trip should be made in the morning – it's not so hot then and your camera can click almost non-stop capturing the colourful and lively floating market of the village Ywama.

The motor boats stand ready for boarding at Yaunghwe and can take 8 people, and are not so very uncomfortable. "Tourist Burma", the national tourist agency, which took first class care of our group, had made all the arrangements; not only would lunch be waiting for us in a bamboo hut on one of the canals leading to the lake on our return, but we were also presented with an umbrella for the trip – equally important in rain or sun.

Then the fast, loud – because of the outboard motor – trip could start. It was my good fortune to sit next to Mya Mya, our very charming and just as knowledgeable Burmese guide – a lot of the information included here came from her; she moved as gracefully and elegantly as any Paris mannequin in her longyi, and was a favourite subject for the gentlemen photographers in our party.

The actual size of the lake can't really be estimated from Yaunghwe, the oldest and most important of the some 200 Intha settlements at, or on, the water; it is surrounded by a wide strip, up to 5 kilometres (3 miles) wide in some places, of water plants, wild hya-

cinths, reeds and mud. The Inthas have cut their canals through the surface of this thicket. We travel down one to reach the waters of the lake.

Although the Inle Lake, with its low depths, lies in the settlement area of the Shan people, the 100,000 Inthas who live here are the real "People of the Lake". As early as in the 15th century they fled their original homeland near Tavoy in the South Burmese Tenasserim, when war raged there between Burma and Thailand. The Inle Lake not only offered a new home, it also provided a living.

These Inthas are the famous leg rudderers; balancing on one leg on the bows of their small, squat, boats, they control the rudder with the other, leaving both hands free for the bow nets. And they display their skills in competitions on festive occasions.

Small dots on the wide waters become quickly larger and take shape as we speed towards them. Six fishing boats have collected at one point where there are shoals of fish, we were able to take our time photographing the men at work. But catches of catfish, eels or carp are not the only delicacies which deck the Inthas' tables. They also became famous for their floating gardens which supply them with various kinds of vegetables – and lots of tomatoes. Water plants and mud are the bases for what later become gardens; with a layer of arable humus building up over decades – the birth of a floating island. The gardeners slice of pieces and punt these over the lake to their villages, gardening and tilling then takes place from boats. There is however another method of winning land. Reed mats are bound together and mud, drawn from the bed of the lake, piled on top.

Mya Mya appeared to be at home when we finally reached the picturesque village of Ywama. She knew and greeted almost all the inhabitants of the bamboo houses built on small islands. For the Inthas have also proved themselves masters in the art of building: structures on piles have walls of spliced bamboo in artistic designs. In between, throngs of boats – the only means of transport for the natives – a miniature Venice in Burma, created by the fairly affluent Inthas. In one house we were led to a typical cigar "factory", where girls, on piece work, make the famour "Cheroots", those thick Burmese cigars which particularly elderly women puff with inimitable self-confidence. Wages are low, but the atmosphere gay as the strangers burst in on this idyllic scene of rural work. Naturalness, born of spontaneity, not only at the factory, but also at the floating market of this village; not spruced up in best bib and tucker for the tourists' benefit like that in Bangkok; but simple, very colourful. Asia of the 19th century: 30 to 40 boats loaded with fruits and vegetables. Market women huddled under their woven peaked hats out of the burning sun. And one old lady gets very annoyed when, after haggling for ages, I don't take the bunch of bananas offered after all. Make sure you have plenty of film for this market.

Right next door to the bustle of activity on the water, the not very remarkable pagoda, Phaung Daw U; nevertheless it plays a major role in the lives of the Inthas. It houses namely those five figures of Buddha which are said to have been brought from Malaysia by the widely travelled Pagan king, Alaungsithu in the 12th century; when they were hidden in a cave near the lake quite possibly they were still recognisable as Buddhas. Today however,

Vegetable market in Mandalay. The Golden City according to Kipling.

they are becoming – in their place of honour under the umbrella in the main hall, almost shapeless bundles, which make it difficult for even experts to see in them Buddhas. The reason for their surprising increase in girth; over the centuries the faithful have packed them in gold foil.

Apparently this has not affected their holy powers in any way and they are displayed once a year. During the festival of Phaung Daw U (also called Karaweik festival) four of the five Buddhas are punted over the lake on splendidly decorated royal barges to 13 villages; which then hope for rich harvests in return. Bookings have to be made years in advance to experience this spectacle of brilliant colour.

Various experts are of the opinion that the Inle Lake is doomed. It is silting up and the profusion of water hyacinths are threatening to choke it completely. If suitable counter measures are not put into practice soon, Burma will be poorer by one more tourist attraction in the Shan Mountains. Most tourists reach Inle Lake by air, only thirty minutes flight from Mandalay, about twice as long as that from Rangoon to Heho. This small airport which lies around 40 kilometres (24.8 miles) from both the lake and Taunggyi is the starting point for excursions. Small buses, in really good condition, transport tourists from there to Taunggyi, the major Shan town, which boasts a fine museum and also offers a most appealing open-air market. Members of various tribes meet here every five days to offer their mainly agricultural, products to the town's total population 40,000, housewives. The colourful and imaginative national dress of some of the 30 tribes of the Shan territories can be seen in the museum.

Less official, and in all liklihood that much more profitable, is the night market in the town. It's rumoured to be the main source of smuggled wares from Thailand, in other words the centre of a type of economy which is gaining more and more significance in Burma, whereby officialdom, for the most part, turns a blind eye. Not that much could be done anyway; from Taunggyi the road leads to Kengtung in the Golden Triangle which is supplied with goods and products from Thailand; the road however is controlled by Shan rebels who are alleged to have organised a regular system of tolls on smuggled goods – boat engines and spare parts for instance are high on the hit list.

At 1,450 metres (4,757 ft) above sea level the climatically favourable site of Taunggyi was already much appreciated by the officers of Her Brittanic Majesty. In the 19th century they became something resembling the city fathers and bequeathed to present day tourists the "Taunggyi Strand", briefly referred to as Taunggyi Hotel. Nestling among pine and eucalyptus trees, the hotel radiates that solidly comfortable colonial atmosphere, which is not always something to be regarded as positive; one looks for 5 star comfort here in vain.

But you don't have to pack your bags in Heho for a trip to Inle Lake. Trips to Kalaw are also organised here (some 40 kilometres / 25 miles away). This one time "hill station" of British colonial servants, also blessed with a moderate climate, is dominated by brightly dressed Palaung who have settled in this area. And another 40 kilometres (25 miles) further on from Kalaw – in the territory settled by the Danu – the cult caves of the Pindya are becoming more and more a favourite destination for travel groups. Many statues of Buddha were set up by the faithful in these natural caves on the Shan plateau; an ancient cult practice which probably dates back to Indian influence and which is also seen in some parts of Thailand (at the Kok and Kwae rivers for instance).

As we travelled back around lunchtime over the lake to Yaunghwe a slight drizzle started, the mountains hid behind a curtain of cloud and rain and the shores disappeared. Boats coming towards us tore vague shapes in the grey shroud before disappearing just as quickly into the mist behind us. The previously so appealing lake had slipped behind a ghostly mask.

Crouched under the welcome umbrellas we longed for an end to the four hour excursion. But then as we stood at Heho Airport after lunch the familiar blue of the Burmese heavens arched over us once more.

And Mya Mya had reserved the best seats for us on the waiting aircraft. We were flying to Mandalay.

Shellacked

It is hardly ever lacking in tourists' homebound baggage; lacquered work from Burma or Thailand. Light, handy, decorative too, the ideal souvenir, one based on a tradition almost 4,000 years old. The art of lacquering was already practiced in the ancient empires of China and probably became widespread in Thailand in the first half of this millenium; the art spread from there to Burma.

Basic product is the lac (sap) or resin of the Lac tree (Rhus vernicifera) which is tapped almost in the same way as rubber – a horizontal slash is made in the bark and the resin caught in a small cup as it oozes out. Originally whitish, transparent, the sap becomes darker and thicker, then hard and black. Thinly spliced bamboo forms the core of every lacquered vessel; coated with lacquer the frame work is hung to dry for the first time. A mixture of lacquer, ash from burned rice husks, sawdust or cow dung serves in smoothing

the framework which is then smoothed once more on a type of potter's wheel. Then the craftsman applies a new coat of black lacquer until the object is completely smooth. A final coat is applied, mainly red, and this is smoothed again. Then, after drying, is engraved in such a way that the black undercoat shines through in the chosen design. Valuable items have up to three coats of lacquer applied in colour. The whole is then highly polished with oil. Alternating working and drying phases lead to a complicated procedure for completion of just one object and several months are needed to finish a really valuable piece. Boxes, cups, plates and other objects ranging in size up to that of a painting can best be bought by the tourist at Chiang Mai in Thailand and in Burma in the vicinity of Pagan. A visit to a so-called lacquering factory is always rewarding for then one can watch the craftsmen at work.

Make-up Burmese Style and the Hindlegs of an Elephant

If one didn't know better then one would view with astonishment the Burmese women's practice of smearing themselves with clay; face and arms are coated in a yellowish paste even then when the ladies sparkle in their festive longyis with all their still visible charms on show. And even the children are frequently smothered in the same way. There is however a very logical explanation: this yellow paste dries on the skin, smooths and soothes at the same time, and is not clay or any other unappetising goo. What it is, is the ground bark of the Thanaka tree. The Burmese ladies are firmly convinced that nature supplied them not only with a first class protection from the sun but also a cooling make-up at budget prices; a fine, delicate, perfume increases the beneficial effects of the paste, whose colour provides an attractive contrast to the brown skins. Thanaka wood is a must at every Burmese market.

The velvety skins of the Burmese women moved even the formerly hostile Thais to literary flights of praise; the elegance of the Indians and the skins of the Burmese were held up to Thai women as ideals of feminine beauty.

Traditional dress almost certainly contributes to the highly appealing impression made by the ladies but the men wear longyi too, an ankle length skirt or sarong but in this case called a pasoe, and preferably of a checked material, whilst the women show a preference for brilliant flower patterns. Pasoes are knotted at the front and longyis knotted at the side, though by no means a Gordian knot; the light clothing, ideal for tropic climes which so flatteringly outlines the figure, is reslung round the hips several times a day, to prevent any involuntary striptease. There is always still an element of uncertainty however; where was this style of dress created? Which people was the first to discover this fashion which spread throughout Asia and the Pacific? The Indonesians call the garment a sarong, the South Sea islanders have named it a pareo and the Turkish use almost the same expression as the Burmese, namely londschi.

For this reason many suspect that the clothing started on a long victorious campaign in Turkey and reached Burma relatively late via India.

Go, go – Girl

She's called Lek, and she's tiny. Born 22 years ago as the sixth child of a debt ridden rice farmer in the north of Thailand. Hardly able to stand on her own two feet, she was expected to take over a whole list of responsibilities ranging from looking after the younger brothers and sisters to collecting firewood, work which started early in the morning and ended late at night. Lek was never young, never a child.

School was an inaccessible luxury. Later, with a lot of effort, she was able to scratch her name in Thai letters. But Lek had a good figure and a pretty face. And she was determined to cash in on them. First in her own village, where she turned the heads of the young men. One swallowed the bait and they were married. At the wedding feast, strictly in accordance with Buddhistic rites the "Little One's" (Lek = little) world was still in order. Then the baby announced it's arrival; the debts on the house and urgently needed basic commodities, threatened to swamp the stricken pair. Then the baby was there, but the husband no longer. He had, nothing unusual in this country, cast a look around for someone else.

At this point at the very latest Lek's future had reached a dead end. The baby was put into its grandparent's care. Lek went to an agent. For a few Baht he took over the young woman's affairs, put her on a bus in the direction of Bangkok and pressed a note bearing several addresses into her hand.

The street was always the same in all the addresses: Patpong. And Bangkok's some 300,000 prostitutes had one more colleague.

On festive occasions the women wear an Eingyi over their longyis, a transparent top elaborately decorated with precious stones, natural riches of the country, sparking in all imaginable colours. Not quite so colourful on the other hand are the men, although their courageousness as far as colourful clothing is concerned is unbroken. Chinese tailors fostered the upper clothing which takes the form of a grey or black jacket (Taik ingyi) with, as the finishing touch, festive headgear. This Gaung-baung, a cap with a pointed crown is bought today ready-made and only worn on special occasions, with various shapes indicating the rank of the wearer.

It's not the hand that rocks the cradle that rules the world, but the one that holds the purse strings. The Burmese woman, as family treasurer, would at most lift an astonished eye-brow at the manner in which emancipation is practiced in our parts of the world. This is by no means intended as a judgement of the merits of either method. The woman of the "Golden Land" are tradition bound. There is no way open to them to a career in politics or executive positions in business.

For the most part they are still happy in their role as mistress of the household, as treasurer of family funds. This

It could have been a lot worse however. The agent was not a bad lot without connections. And with her appearance Lek really did tread the boards, which in Patpong certainly don't mean the world.

She is now a Go-go girl, on show from six in the evening until midnight. Swinging her hips and legs to hot music – admittedly skillfully – and the fact that she only wears a teeny-weeny bikini doesn't bother her – not any more. It's what the men want. Thais and lots and lots of foreign tourists.

Almost every evening the inevitable happens: Lek "falls in love" with one of the guests. After she has finished work they go hand in hand to one of the discreet hotels close by. And there too Lek will give of her best to satisfy her "friend". If she is lucky he'll make her a gift of a pile of Baht which she sends, keeping hardly anything for herself, to her family in the North, where her daughter in the meantime has just reached school age. Lek's work makes school possible, has made life easier for the whole family.

Lek has long been resigned to the fact that she won't marry again. No Thai would have her, and she is still just a little bit afraid of farangs (foreigners). Still she's happy that her daughter and family are prospering, and after all dancing is not too strenuous.

She is a Go-go girl. Or should one say go, go girl! Go – the question is where?

By the way Lek earns round 3,000 Baht a month, about the same as a teacher.

will almost certainly change as Western influence becomes stronger. On the other hand changes are already becoming obvious in Thailand where the modern Thai woman no longer accepts her role as the "hindlegs of the elephant" without protest. She is still, it is true, committed, between tradition and progress, to follow in the footsteps of her husband, although however "freedom through the pill" is opening up new paths.

Financial independence has joined forces with sexual. Women occupy major posts in business and claim equality not only in black and white on a government decree. But they still have a long way to go before that equality guaranteed on paper becomes a fact of life, particularly in rural areas. Nevertheless it appears as if the previously so docile hindlegs of the elephant are ready to go their own way.

Risky Ballet

They move like artistic dancers and attempt to hurt their partners; in five three minute rounds, they hammer each other with their fists, butt with their heads, knees or shoulders into each other, kick. Apart from judo holds and wrestling, everything and anything is allowed to knock the other off his feet. Thai boxing, a fascinating mixture of ballet elegance and destructive lack of restraint which degenerated from the art of self-defence during the Ayutthaya era to become a competitive spectator sport. But even today Thai boxing finds ardent fans among natives and tourists alike; which is proven by the daily events which alternate between the two Bangkok stadiums – Lumpini and Rajadamnern.

The whole exhibition starts off harmlessly enough. Both fighters enter the ring differing in no way in appearance from other prize boxers. Gloves and shorts are the same. But these boxers wear a magic headband dedicated by their teachers, with, more often than not, a talisman concealed beneath.

Before the fight starts they perform a slow dance with which they express a stylised form of their skills, accompanied by a four piece orchestra on drums, flutes and cymbals. Then the blows fly. Attacks are introduced with kicks. No part of the opponent's body is taboo; betting odds are shouted in the crowd, which spurs on the current favourite. The music increases in tempo to a frenzy. The boxers did not wear gloves in the past. They just wrapped their hands in hemp ropes and the fight only ended when one of the fighters just wasn't able to stand up. If the favoured champion loses, the disappointed punters comfort themselves with a bottle of Mekong whisky and hope for better luck in the next match.

In a Jumbo to see the Jumbos

As if they knew what an impressive sight they made, around 80 elephants formed up to march over the wide-spreading, disused airfield of Surin in east Thailand. All are wearing the trappings of war, splendid harnesses, yellow and red, richly embroidered caparisons, silver trimmed saddles, truly a majestic sight. Highpoint and finale of the annual parade of elephants which takes place each November here.

Mahouts come from all over Thailand, trainers and riders, with their elephants to Surin; for on the two days in November when the spectacle attracts numerous tourists and thousands of Thais, there is plenty of money to be earned. After each show on Saturday and Sunday (starting at 9 a.m. and finishing at noon), the mahouts offer elephant rides at 50 Baht for 20 minutes. A city sight-seeing tour Surin style.

Perhaps the most fascinating thing of all is the way the traffic comes to a complete standstill in the streets of central Surin because the Jumbos claim right of way as their privilege – and who would argue! Baby elephants seek protection under their mothers when a truck drives past too quickly; traffic rules go overboard in Surin on these two days. The show put on by the trained worker elephants is spellbinding, and during the parade of the war elephants which follows photographers let their cameras run hot, but in spite of this many a tourist is in some uncomfortable way reminded of the travelling circuses at home.

The atmosphere in the town before and after the show at the airfield, more than compensates for the long trip to east Thailand. Large numbers of people are underway all night from Bangkok by special trains and bus tourists too have a long road behind them, until they stand in the admiring crowds round the elephants and there is something like wonder written all over their faces.

The close relationship with elephants in both Thailand and Burma is traditional, but although the Thai mahouts still give their elephants commands in Burmese, the animals themselves have almost become extinct in Burma, only found in the wilds of almost inaccessible jungles (around 6,000), otherwise the water buffalo has to a great extent replaced this "tractor of the jungle" (some 3,000 working elephants), and even on the Irrawaddy, which after all means Elephant River, they no longer exist.

In Thailand on the other hand the number of pachyderms is estimated at some 14,000, but in spite of this they are still a threatened species; at the end of the 18th century they are said to have numbered 200,000. They have however still remained a symbol of good fortune for the royal house, al-

though this only applies to the rare white elephants. One of these albinoes can be seen at Bangkok zoo. And at one time in the past there was even an elephant war between the two countries – the elephant was included in the Thai coat of arms until 1916 – they robbed each other of white elephants.

There are several elephant schools in Thailand which the tourist can visit. Most are in the North and the admiring visitor can learn there that the size of an elephant can be reckoned exactly from the circumference of its foot. Thus elephant hunters of bygone days only had to measure the diameter of the spoor and multiply it by three to know what size of animal they were hunting and form the hunting party accordingly.

There are still more fascinating things one can learn; for instance that formerly there was only one mahout to an elephant, and the animal only accepted this one person as its master, some would say friend. Nowadays two mahouts are responsible for each young jumbo, mainly for financial reasons, since the animal as a rule lives longer than a human, so its capacity for work could be better exploited this way.

The jumbos are trained for their work in the jungles at an early age and training usually starts when the animal is around four years old. Fully trained animals do not work all day; they suffer in intense heat and are given the afternoon off in the shade of the giant jungle trees. In the mornings they more than make up for their afternoon siesta, by displaying enormous feats of strength, towing huge teak trunks on chains to more accessible centrally located collection points in the jungles.

What is impressively demonstrated at the Surin parade is the elephant's above average ability to learn. While two teams of six elephants with riders try to score against each other with an outsize ball, the name Beckenbauer croaks, too loudly, out of a scratchy loudspeaker several times, but in spite of their ability they are still not quite in the same class.

One hundred and eighty (180!) Thai soldiers measure their strength against that of the most powerful bull in a tug-of-war. All their efforts are in vain. Although the animal at first shows some signs of weakening in the hindquarters, it wins in the end.

And it really is the end, Surin returns to normal, the elephants return to the jungle, and the tourists either back to Bangkok or to a Jumbo, and home.

Maung Tin becomes a Priest

Farewell to childhood. Buddhistic rites with the roots in ancient cults surrounding puberty. Parents humbly offering their sons food and being thankful for its acceptance. Maung Tin is nine years old – and was ordained as a priest only a few hours ago in Buddhist Burma.

The village close to historic Pagan groans under the searing heat of the midday sun. People doze in the shade of the few trees, or have sought refuge in the relative cool of their homes. The place seems empty of life.

But it only seems so. In front of a tent richly decorated with flowers there is pulsing life. Women in festive dress and men, hardly less colourful, among some dozen gaily embellished ox-carts; the animals – all white – have also been decorated with great care, and don't appear to have appreciated this attention too much. They remain stolidly impervious to the music and bustle around them. Maybe they have taken part in more than one Shinbyu ceremony already…

For Maung Tin and 15 other boys however something unique is taking place, something which is, at the same time, a beginning and an end, a gateway into the future. With this ceremony of shaving heads (Shinbyu) they become members of the Shangha, the community of Buddhistic monks. Embedded in the social tradition of faith Maung Tin's path will be, from now on, accompanied by Buddhism. His childhood is over.

Days and weeks of, at times frantic, preparation lie behind him, and now he sits with the other novices on a dais in the tent. The feet of the children, wrapped in robes woven through with gold thread, do not touch the floor. As if aware of the solemnity of the occasion they stare before them; under the red-gold paper crown and heavy shawl trimmed with Talmi, the children have the appearance of fragile dolls.

A group of musicians intones solemn music in the background, in front of the novices, relatives and invited guests cower on mats on the ground.

Phi and Nat – A Ghost House

Chao Thi lives in almost every Thai house and more, he has a house within a house, the Sala Phra Phum! True his house is more of a cottage, but still a house for spirits. Chao Thi is the good spirit of every Thai family.

Even today spirits and ghosts dominate their surroundings although more than 90% of all Thais and Burmese are followers of Therawada Buddhism (see special chapter on religions). Monks and teachers have for centuries skillfully woven them into this religion, only considered an imperfect stage on the way to the higher wisdom of Buddhism.

The Thais call their innumerable supernatural forces "Phi", with the Burmese they are known as "Nat" (Sanskrit, Nath = Lord, Master). Before the rise of Buddhism, Phi and Nat predominated, determining and ruling the religious cult, animism. Science calls this a natural religion.

Not a rare occurrence: while the comfortable bus wends its way over a well plastered mountain road in the north of Thailand, the driver suddenly takes his hands from the wheel, places them on his forehead and bows. The reason for this strange and risky gesture? We had just passed a spirit house and the driver had humbly greeted Phi; completely trusting in Phi to watch over the bus for the few seconds when no hand was on the steering wheel. Really up-to-date drivers content themselves today with a short blast on the horn.

The spirit world of Thailand and Burma is confusing. The number of these supernatural forces hard to determine. They are not only spread all over the earth, they also appear as angels in Heaven or demons in Hell; there are good and evil amongst them, some settled in one place, others wandering. And all are paid tribute. Which ensures help from the good when in need and keeping the evil at bay.

Strict rules govern the building, erection and function of Chao Thi's house. It must be raised above the ground and great care must be taken that at no time the shadow of the real house falls on it; and vice versa, the spirit house must not cast shadows on the big house, since this after all also accomodates Buddha's altar.

Almost every day the conscientious family brings its domestic ghost tributes; small clay horses to mark succesful business deals for instance and every guest is well advised to pay respects to the house spirit before taking leave.

In this way Phi and Nat have become to Buddhism what the saints are in Christianity; helpers in need, with responsibility for specific events. The success of a trip depends just as much on their benevolence as do harmonious family life, success at school or at work and of course health. Even the gamblers have their own special spirit; Lak Muang, influential patron of all natives of Bangkok is considered the patron of gamblers too; and the lottery ticket sellers in front of his "temple" do a roaring trade.

In Burma too Buddhism has entered into a symbiosis with natural religions. There, the Nats distinguish themselves from demons, witches and other ghosts and spirits in that the Nats are the spirits of Burmese mythology, demi-gods, once living, exceptional human beings.

There are three recognisable groups; the 37 superior Nats, with the King of Spirits, Sakkra, taking the lead, followed by the group of nature Nats and finally the Devas.

While ordinary Nats and nature Nats can be both good or evil, the Devas are without exception moral and good; these have their origins in the world as seen by Buddhists. But "The Lord of the Great Mountain" protects all houses in Burma too, from his own cottage.

The murmuring in the tent dies off as a group of at least 20 monks press their way through the crowd to the dais. They lower themselves as a band of orange behind the novices. When the fathers of the boys offer them refreshments with deep bows, this is the signal for all to be served.

Maung Tin's great moment comes immediately after the feast; he and the other novices are divested of their splendid robes and that monk who will care for the boy during the next weeks in the monastery, starts to shave his head. Parents have spread white cloths out next to their sons to catch the black locks; at one time the shorn hair was buried close to the pagoda but today it is taken home by the parents.

Then Maung Tin is dressed by his monastic teacher in the saffron robe of the monk. From now on he is a "Son of Buddha" and takes the vows of his order before the monks; long Plai texts (simplified Sanskrit) are sung and the new Ponchis (begging monks) are given the few possessions permitted in the monastery; sandals, fan, sunshade, the black begging bowl on a belt.

Even his name is left by Maung Tin in the hot, stifling, tent. When tomorrow he goes for the first time to the village to collect food for the monastery, barefoot as Buddha was, with eyes downcast, then his mother too will kneel before him and thank him for accepting her tribute; her son has helped her to achieve a better Karma.

Events of the day before the ceremony were more worldly. Together with the others and accompanied by the villagers and the orchestra Maung Tin could play at being a prince – for a few hours at least – splendidly robed the boys were escorted on the decorated ox-carts (in the past it had to be white horses) through the village. The road from home to homelessness, from riches to poverty, which was once taken by Buddha is thus followed symbolically.

Every Burmese, male and female, spends several months at some time in life at a monastery or convent; most of them several times, to follow the way of the Enlightened through meditation to Nirvana. The doors are open to all, at all times. Abbots and other high

Shinbyu ceremony of the young monks

ranking monks enjoy great respect among the people, they remain lifelong in the monastery and bound to the strict rules of their order.

The same applies to Thailand where ascetic wandering monks of the Tudong school, in their typical brown robes, are specially privileged.

Monasteries in Thailand and Burma perform several functions and are much more than just religious communities. The monastery is often the only opportunity to attend school given to the young of poor families. The sick come and place themselves in the healing care of the monks, the poor are fed and – when they enter the order – given a home. The monastery as a form of old age insurance. A substitute for government aid. In Burma alone there are some 13,000 monasteries with around 250,000 monks.

Thailand

System of Government:
Constitutional monarchy, the King is representative head of state and religious patron.

Administration:
Division into 71 provinces (Changwad), the Provincial Governor is appointed by the Minister of the Interior and responsible to this same. The provinces are subdivided into 551 districts (Amphoes) and these in turn into 5,042 sub-districts (Tambol) and around 44,000 villages, in which the village elders govern in cooperation with the head of the village temple.

National Defence:
The King is Supreme Commander and nominal Field Marshall. Two years conscription for men. The army numbers 95,000 in times of peace (70,000 reservists), the police 40,000, the air force 25,000 and the navy around 20,000. Military equipment is for the most part American. A SEATO member since 1955.

Judicial System:
Since Thailand was never a colony it was in a position to develop its own judicial system. Rama V Chulalongkorn pressed for development of legislation and jurisdiction resembling that of France. Ministry of Justice was established in 1922. In force at present is the Civil Code of 1935 and the Penal Code of 1957. Supreme Court is in Bangkok.

Education:
Compulsory schooling for children from the age of 7 was introduced in 1921, for a minimum of four years. At present, schooling is divided into 4 years elementary school and three years at senior level, then two periods of each three years at senior or comprehensive schools with two years at high school as a preliminary to university study. There are today 7 universities and technical colleges, the oldest being Chulalongkorn University in Bangkok which was founded in 1917. Elementary schooling is free, private schools charge in some cases high fees. In rural areas a major role is played now as in the past by the Buddhistic monasteries and convents. Around 30% of the population is illiterate.

Major Museums:
Bangkok: National Museum with a first class exhibition of cultural development, National Library.
Ayutthaya: National Museum,
Sukhothai: National Museum, probably with the highest standards in the country,
Lopburi: National Museum,
Phimai: Museum near the Khmer Temple with, for example, first class sculptures.

Burma

System of Government:
Socialist republic under a president based on the Constitution of 1974.

Administration:
The state comprises Central Burma (7 administrative areas), the Shan State (Federal State), the States of the Kachin, Kayah and Karen and the special territory of the Chin: each state has its own state government; princes have been stripped of power in the Shan

States. Border territories of the Shan and Kachin states are subject to military rule. Administrative districts of Mandalay, Arakan, Magwe, Irriwaddy, Pegu, Sagaing and Tenasserim are divided into 14 districts and these in turn divided into boroughs and villages; security committees appointed by the central government have decisive powers.

National Defence:
General conscription for men and women has still not been put into practice. The army numbers 140,000, the navy 6,000 and the air force 6,500. Equipment is for the most part British and American. Under a Treaty of Friendship, entered into in 1960 with the People's Republic of China, Burma may not enter into any military pacts.

Judicial System:
Law is based on British law adopted in India. Special rights for national minorities. Social laws passed in 1951–54. Supreme Court is in Rangoon since 1962.

Education:
Compulsory elementary school from the age of 6, theoretically for a total of 9 years. Private schools still occupy a major position. Two universities (Rangoon founded in 1920) and 29 high schools and colleges. Illiteracy rate is between 30% and 42% (figures vary depending on source).

Major Museums:
Nyaung U/Pagan: new museum with some excellent Buddhistic sculptures; next door – traditional puppet theatre.

Rangoon: National Museum with the "Lion Throne" of Mandalay: Museum at the "Institute for Advanced Buddhistic Studies" with palm leaf manuscripts and Buddhistic sculptures.

Mandalay: National Library and Museum, not very interesting.

Taunggyi: Museum exhibiting tribal dress of various tribes.

Accord with some Dissonance – Historical Background

Picture of a marriage of convenience which has lasted a thousand years – they don't, it is true, have to pull together, but on the other hand, what would they do without each other? That is the history of Thailand and Burma since they entered the historical picture. Togetherness often enough turned into a head-on collision, truly a love-hate relationship. But bound by fate, under all circumstances. Almost at the same time in history they set foot on that territory which they today, as independent peoples, call home; almost at the same time in history they established their realms – and were promptly at loggerheads; their cultures spring from the same sources; Hinayana Buddhism and Indian and Chinese customs fed their cultures and soon entered into competition. Today they avoid each other as much as possible, but are still inextricably bound. Accord with dissonance.

Before the Thai and Burmese migrated towards the southern sun there was a veil over the history of those regions in which they later settled. This pre-historical era ended in Burma in the 11th century according to our calender, whilst Thailand emerged earlier from the shroud of historical darkness. According to latest knowledge the north of Thailand was already settled in 9000 B.C. by Negristic tribes, small, dark-skinned, with short, tightly curled, hair; and Burmese soil has already surrendered stone artefacts (arrow heads etc.), which were used by these Negritoes. They were in all probability assimilated, or driven out, by Malayans, for whom Thailand and Burma were nothing more than wayside stops on their long migration through South-east Asia to the Indonesian, Philippine and finally, Pacific Islands. All nomadic tribes of the Stone and Iron Ages who left no permanent traces on the plains of the Chao Phaya and Irrawaddy.

Fascinating uncertainty: on the plateau close to the Thai town of Udorn Thani in the north-east, highly developed bronze relics and painted clay vessels have been excavated; experts from all parts of the world sing the praises of the village Ban Chiang where the earth surrenders most archaeological finds, probably due to the fact that thousands of years ago there was an enormous burial ground close to the village. Many theories concerning the early settlement of Thailand and Burma, which have been accepted until now as scientific fact, will have to be revised because of Ban Chiang; at present there are still no plausible explanations.

They were called Mon in Burma and Thailand, Khmer in Thailand and Pyu in Burma, those were the peoples with which both countries trod the stage of history. The Pyu and Mon are members of the Deutero-Malayan family. (Early Malayans today predominant in Indonesia and the Philippines.) Sometime between 300 B.C. and the New Age the Pyu (Chinese: Piao) reached west Burma, while the Mon pushed on to the Irrawaddy Delta, Sittang and Salween and also settled along the Chao Phaya. Around the same time, the Khmer, related to the Mon, in all probability set foot on the soil of Thailand and Kampuchea (Cambodia). Around 500 A.D. the die is cast; the Pyu from the central Asian steppes create the first realm on Burmese soil – Sri Ksetra, close to present day Prome and Halingyi in the Shwebo District – the Mon become active in Thailand; south and central Thailand are ruled by the Dvaravati kingdom, the north by Hairpujaya. Lopburi appears in annals for the first time as capital of Dvaravati. The first roots of the Khmer realm are planted, to reach full bloom between the 11th and 13th centuries, on the territory of presentday Kampuchea.
But the Mon too have become active, politically and religiously on Burmese soil. Their Thai settlements having only existed for a very short period as a loose confederation; they spread towards the north and in the 9th century establish a realm with Pegu as the major city. Already 1,200 years earlier they had put out feelers towards Ashoka's realm in India from their port Thaton, "Goldland" they called their country which they opened to Hinduism and later, more intensely, Hinayana Buddhism. In Thailand, as in Burma, these Mon sowed seeds of culture even when their realms, all of them, only existed for short periods of time.

The end of the Pyu on Burmese soil comes from the north, their Sri Ksetra, with its clay brick architecture, is the first of those early kingdoms of Burma and Thailand to fall victim to the storming Thais, others then fell to the Birmans. In 832 A.D. the armies of Nan-chao from the north-east, invade Burma with their Thai and Shan tribes, destroy Sri Ksetra and carry off thousands of captives; the end of the Pyu as a people.

From a military aspect the Mon fare no better on Thai and Burmese ground. Sudhammavati, Ramanyadesa and finally Dvaravati were the realms driven out by the Birmans and / or Thais by the 13th century at latest. As opposed to the Pyu however the Mon remain in those areas settled even after the end of their political existence, and their level of culture led them to become the teachers of their conquerers. This is testified to today by Buddhism and the numerous sacral structures which clearly bear the mark of Mon architects. War drums in the 8th / 9th centuries; the Birmans reach the fruitful rice fields of Burma on the Irrawaddy (central). They have already long foot marches behind them through the desolate west China and the wilderness of east Tibet when the southern sun exerts an irresistible pull. Toughness was the result of the long migration – and they know how to put it to good use. Pagan is built, Anawrahta (1044–1077) the first ruler of this dynasty under which Burma reaches the peak of its culture and history. From Pagan the Birmans control the plains of the Irrawaddy, the valley of the Sittang and major trade routes between China and India.

Anawrahta must have been a determined man. In a lightning war, using his war elephants, he defeats the Mon's Thaton and carries home in triumph 30,000 captives including the Royal Family, learned men, architects, monks and craftsmen. Thirty white elephants bear the "Tripitaka" on their backs; with this written record the ancient form of Buddhism takes root at the court of Pagan. Around 5,000 temples and pagodas remain as powerful memorials of the peak of Hinayana power when this dynasty comes to an end. Pagan enters the annals of history as the "City of four million Pagodas". A highly developed system of irrigation canals provided the financial backbone of the kingdom.

Golden Era under the "Warrior King"; Kyanzittha (1084–1113) builds the Ananda Temple after he had crushed a Mon uprising; a ship loaded with treasure is despatched to Bengal to pay for repairs of the Mahabodhi Temple at Bodhgaya; language and culture of the Mons complement the robust pragmatism of the Birmans.

Rise to power – from nothing: Burma was never again to reach those political or cultural heights reached during the first Pagan realm. But, after eleven rulers the dynasty is exhausted, the end comes quickly. Kublai Khan's hordes of Mongolian horsemen, the perfect war machine of the times, have overrun the Thai kingdom of Nan-chao and stand with their emissaries before the mighty gates of Pagan. King Narathilhapate refuses the tributes demanded – in 1287 the Mongols rule Pagan, Narathihapate's son, Kyawswa, is enthroned as puppet ruler. Chaos is the result for the next 250 years.

As the star of the first Birman kingdom sinks, that of the Thais rises as rapidly as a comet. They also have long migrations behind them as they finally appear in what is to become their home. Their probable, original settlements around the Yangste had long been abandoned (see separate chapter), when they at last, around 650, establish the first known Nan-chao kingdom in West Yunnan under the famous ruler, Pi-lo-ko. This "Southern Land" was administered by an hierarchic organisation of civil servants and thanks to the conscription of all able bodied people, was independent.

However in the 9th century, the dream of complete independence is finally over as Nan-chao becomes liable for tribute to the Chinese Tang Dynasty. Expansionism even after the fall of this dynasty drives the Thais still further south; when Thai Yai (Great Thai), one of the Shan tribes reaches Assam, others follow the Salween and settle in the jungle areas between Burma and Thailand.

The Thai Noi (Lesser Thai) finally appear on the scene in Thailand and Laos. In 1253, Nan chao had fallen victim to the armies of Kublai Khan and all the Thai tribes now press further and further south; a migratory movement which had already begun in the 8th century was now moving towards its decisive close. The Thai Noi expel Mon and Khmer, or are assimilated into them, the merger of Mon, Khmer and Thai cultures takes place.

The classic tale of Thailand begins: weak Khmer, politically torpid Mons, have no real defences against the determined Thai rulers; independent Thailand, still thriving today, shows its first faint contours. In 1262 there comes into existence in north Thailand the princedom of Chiang Saen which later, under the name Lan-na (millions of rice fields), is to conquer Haripunjaya (1292) of the Mons, as well as parts of Burma, Laos and southern China. Mangrai is the ruler who 34 years later makes Chiang Mai capital. Centuries of wars with the Burmese follow, who only finally succeed in con-

quering Chiang Mai in 1556 and delivering the death thrust to the Lan-na kingdom.

Further south decisive events are taking place too; in 1238 Sukhothai is established close to the site of present-day Phitsanulok; Thais appear on the scene of South-east Asia as political and economic powers. The birth pangs of a nation. In Sukhothai the foundations are laid for what is to become Siam, and present day Thailand.

In only ten years (1250–1260) this country shakes off the shackles of the Khmer and moves against Burma and Malaysia in daring campaigns; what is left of the Mon realm of Dvaravati, annexed by the Khmer, is integrated. Ram Khamheng ("The Courageous" 1277–1317) becomes the ruling personality. State affairs, power politics and religious philosophy complement each other. Thai architecture, freed from the mighty stone edifices of the Khmer, comes into its own. Multi-staged temple roofs demonstrate for the first time that joy of life and religiosity so deeply rooted in the Thai character. Smiling Buddhas with their elegant lines are still considered today exemplary of the art of the land.

Ram Khamheng travels to Beijing (Peking) and brings back not only a Mongolian princess as wife, but also Chinese craftsmen who introduce the art of firing clay, into Thailand. Almost as an afterthought, he creates the first Thai alphabet and declares Hinayana Buddhism the national religion. He is revered as a god by his subjects, although – according to legends – audiences were granted to all requesting them. Perhaps the close bonds between King and subjects which still distinguishes Thailand today, were forged then.

Sukhothai was only to exist some 200 years. Immediately after the death of Ram Khamheng, the decline started; disputes among the single princedoms and neglect of affairs of state mark the end. The political and cultural influence exerted on Thailand's road to the present remains undisputed. Sukhothai was the beginning.

Climax in the twilight of decline: the history of Ayutthaya begins with a natural disaster and ends with one of war. Floods in the city of U Thong force the local ruler to move his court to Ayutthaya. Two years later (1349) this same ruler seizes rule of the dying Sukhothai and as Rama Thibodi I, (1350–1369) rings in the "Golden Age" of Thailand in that he establishes the kingdom of Ayutthaya (1349–1767). A golden age however which was to smelt to become the lowest point in Thai history in the smoke of Burmese plunderers.

Rama Thibodi's rule is brilliant, as is that of his successor. Under the name Siam, the kingdom becomes known even in Europe; history is full of heroic deeds and great kings, art is flourishing. Ayutthaya, built on an island at the junction of three rivers, is to become a major influence in South-east Asia for four centuries, is to make the Thais a leading nation. After a siege lasting seven months even the mighty gates of Angkor, centre of the once dominant Khmer, are opened to them (1431). Only the revitalised Burma scratched at this position. When the glorious Pagan had fallen, the Thai-Shan had, for 250 years, divided the country into small states with changing capitals (Pinya, Sagaing, Ava), the Birmans fled south to the territory of Taungu on the Sittang. A new hub of life came into beeing, but prior to this the Shan adventurer, Wareru, had exploited the helpless position of the small realms, conquered Martaban (1287) and finally had all Lower Burma under his power; the Mon kingdom flourished, and was to exist until 1539; a renaissance of Hinayana Buddhism draws monks and teachers from all parts of South-east Asia.

But then the hour finally comes for the birth of the second Burmese dynasty. Taungu had already claimed the status of kingdom in 1347, but without achieving anything more than purely local significance. This was to change only some 200 years later; Tabinshwehti had himself anointed king of Taungu (1531) and only eight years later he forces the Mon realms of Pegu, then Martaban and Moulmein, followed finally by Pagan and all central and upper Burma under his control.

In 1546 the imposing coronation ceremony takes place at Pegu. "The greatest explosion of human energy Burma has ever experienced" according to the British historian Harvey, as Bayinnaung took the throne as Tabinshwehti's successor. Within only a short space of time he unites the land once more, which had deteriorated into small regions after the death, caused by drunkenness, of Tabinshwehti. He restores the authority of the ruling house in central Burma, Pegu and Prome, subjects Shan and Thai states in the north as far as Chiang Mai (Lan-na realm), exacts tribute from Manipur and even launches a campaign against Luang Prabang in Laos. Between 1560 and 1596 he settles the score with Siam; during the political and military decline of the Mon and Birmanese domains, Ayutthaya had sent troops into Burmese territory. Bayinnaung conquers Ayutthaya, takes the Thai king, Mhinthara-Thirat, prisoner – Burma flexes its muscles and achieves the greatest expansion ever in its history.

Brief greatness; when Bayinnaung dies in 1581, military expansionism exacts its toll; famine spreads. The Siamese fight and regain freedom. Ayutthaya recovers its former glory; the Shan states attack the weak dynasty. And the Thai king, Naresuen, even manages to conquer large areas of the arch-enemy's territories in the West.

Bayinnaung's grandson, Anaukpetlun (1605–1628) is confronted by ruins; only Ava, Upper Burma and a few of the Shan states obey his commands. He too however is a great warrior – in only a few years he has reclaimed central powers. With the difference that now Europe appears on the scene in military campaigns. Vasco da Gama had rounded the Cape of Good Hope in 1498 and thus opened the sea routes to Asia. From this time on European powers take a hand in events in South-east Asia. During this reign Tabinshwehti had already had some 700 Portuguese mercenaries under his command. And it was also Portuguese who settled in Martaban and allied themselves to Arakan and King Mrauk U; there they controlled the coast and maritime trade for a century. And it was also here that the story of Felip de Brito took shape, a story such as was only possible in early colonial Asia; as a cabin boy de Brito had come to Asia and in only a few years had advanced to become ruler of Syriam – he was king of Lower Burma for 13 years.

It was the campaigns of Anaukpetlun which rang the death knell of this success story; with 12,000 soldiers he stormed Syriam, the Portuguese were able to defend themselves for 34 days before their powder ran out. De Brito was impaled on a stake, and took 3 days to die. In 1628 Anaukpetlun also meets with a violent death during a palace revolution.

The days of the Burmese Taungu Dynasty are numbered. In 1752 the last king is taken prisoner by the Mon prince, Binnya Dala, in Ava, which had in the meantime been made capital, and led in triumph to Pegu. There Binnya takes the throne and for all practical purposes it seems as if the Mon – after centuries of disputes with the Birmans – finally have the country in their hands.

In order to remain mobile against Siam, the Mons leave only small garrisons in central and upper Burma. This is exploited by Alaungpaya, the princely son of the Birman Shwebo, in 1752; within a few years he has overrun the Mon realms, levelled Pegu to the ground, carried out an unsuccessful attack on Ayutthaya (1760) and founded the third – and last – Birman kingdom – the Konbaung Dynasty (1752–1885). By the end of this Burma is a British colony.

Son and successor treads in his father's footsteps; Ssinbyushin burns down the rich and powerful Ayutthaya with all its art treasures and scriptures. In 1767 four Chinese attacks are fended off successfully. Manipur and large parts of Assam are occupied and Arakan finally forced to its knees. The fishing village Dagon, until then in the hands of the Mon, had assumed symbolic value for the founder of the dynasty, Alaungpaya; because of the monsoons he had had to break off his campaign against the defeated Mon there; for this reason he renamed the village Yangon (= end of war) – Rangoon had appeared on the maps of Burma, and since 1885 as capital.

Sidetracking to the East; the 17th and 18th centuries were for Siam, governed from the magnificent Ayutthaya, the Golden Age. Already under

King Boromo Trailokanat (1448–1488) that system of rule was established which was to endure until 1932, when it ended after a bloodless coup d'état; deification of the ruler, adopted from the Khmer, who now becomes Bodhisattva with the title "Holy Buddha".

Great ruling personalities such as Naresuen (1574–1605) are capable of coming to terms with the Europeans who are now also appearing in Thailand, and thus preserve independence. The brief period of Burmese superiority is shaken off. Under King Narai (1657–1688) the brilliant Greek adventurer, Constantine Phaulkon, carves out a private position of power as chancellor (prime minister); but as French warships appear on the horizon off the coast of Siam, and shortly afterwards there are disputes with the British East India Company, Phaulkon's assassination is discreetly, but determinedly, planned.

Art and literature reach peaks of perfection. Narai himself becomes famous as author of literary masterpieces. Trade with China and Europe brings affluence, even luxury. Innumerable temples groan under the weight of pure gold, ceremonial barges skim quietly over the waterways; some 400,000 are said to have lived in Ayutthaya when it was at the summit of its glory. France and England vow mutual neutrality; Siam remains free of colonial rule.

Everything flourishes until 1767. After a siege lasting 16 months, after plague, famine and fires, the most beautiful city of South-east Asia falls into the hands of the Burmese under the Konbaung king, Ssinbyushin. The victors run riot; fortresses are razed, temples, monasteries and houses go up in flames; tens of thousands of the inhabitants, including many nobles, are forced into exile. Irreplaceable works of art are destroyed with destruction of the court archives, sources of literature lost forever. After 33 rulers and some 400 years, Ayutthaya had ceased to exist. Climax in the twilight of decline.

A Chinese general, Paya Taksin, survives the Burmese inferno with around 500 men. He is able to flee and successfully takes his revenge; after a short time he has re-conquered Lan-na and Ayutthaya – so utterly destroyed that rebuilding does not take place – and even Laos and Cambodia are once more under Thai rule. In Thonburi, opposite Bangkok, the new capital is established following the traditions of Ayutthaya, but in 1782, Taksin, in the meantime mad with power, falls victim to an officers revolt; the leader, General Chakri, ascends the throne as Rama I Thibodi and thus founds the dynasty which still rules today.

The final chapter of the history of Thailand commences with Bangkok being made the capital.

Under Rama I and Rama II, Siam becomes a major power in South-east Asia once more. Noble edifices such as Wat Po and the Royal Temple are erected and raise the former village to the level of a worthy capital city.

Under Rama IV Mongkut (1851–1868) the one-time Siam opens its doors to the Europeans once more, which had been closed to the outside world after the death of the Ayutthaya King Narai. Treaties are concluded with no less than 14 European countries in order to prevent predominance of any single colonial power. The novel "Anna and the King of Siam", a sentimental love story of the king and the English governess of his children, makes Mongkut immortal in Europe too.

Fairytale Siam is born.

For all that the first really great reformer is to be Rama V Chulalongkorn (1868–1910).

Railway projects and road building, modern forestry and a western oriented educational system, abolishment of slavery and a just system of taxation number among the major changes which distinguish the rule of Chulalongkorn, who occupied the throne of Thailand longer than any other king. At the time of his death in 1910, Siam had undergone immense changes.

Educated in Europe, Rama VI Vajiravudh and Rama VII Rachathipok, continue the policies of the great Chulalongkorn. Nevertheless, time catches up; in 1932 a bloodless military coup breaks the power of the "God King", new legislation transforms Siam into a constitutional monarchy. Disquieting events since then; in addition to a whole series of attempted coups there have been eight successful military uprisings, and a new constitution introduced on nine occasions, and set aside again just as often.

In 1935 Rama VII abdicates in favour of Ananda Mahidol (Rama VIII) who displays a preference for Switzerland as domicile. Nationalistic trends of the military and anti-Chinese tendencies appear to make this advisable. Then in 1939, Siam is passé; the name Thailand becomes official.

When Rama VIII is found shot – the circumstances were never really officially clarified – the country has World War II behind it. At the beginning war had been declared on the allies to avoid Japanese occupation. Since

King Mongkut, or Rama IV.

however Thailand represents an ideal stepping stone to British Malaya, Japanese troops advance on Thailand's territory in 1941. A compensation: the country is assigned parts of Laos and Cambodia. A change of sides in 1944: Thailand swings to the side of the allies and thus survives the war without suffering even when the annexed Laotian and Cambodian lands have to be returned.

"King with sword and saxophone" – Rama IX Bhumipol takes the stage in 1946. He supports the approaches made by the military powers towards the West and pursues a political and economic course which is not always without protest in the country. For this reason there are the first student demonstrations in 1973, when a change of government is accompanied by bloodshed in the streets of Bangkok. The armed forces pull the reins tighter in 1977.

Thailand's membership in SEATO (South-east Asia Treaty Organization / 1955) and the role played by the country in the Vietnam war, provoke new unrest. But; even up to the present the Thai have not lost their thirst for independence, their consciousness of being one people. "Thai Muang" Land of the Free.

Less free and independent of outside influence was the history of Burma from the Konbaung Dynasty to the present. Ssinbyushin had conquered Attuthaya, annexed Chiang Mai and then assigned the regency to Bodawpaya, who in 1782 becomes king of all Burmese. And Bodawpaya did not hesitate long before grasping power. On the advice of his astrologers he not only transfers the capital of his kingdom to Amarapura, close to present day Mandalay, but also conquers Arakan.

This is decisive; the former buffer between British India and Burma is in Burmese hands, disputes along the common borders become more and more frequent, there are border wars. For around 40 years the British lion suffers Burmese troops stepping on its paws, then it bares its claws for the first time; when King Bagyidaw ascends the throne in 1819, the Rajah of Manipur does not attend the coronation; an affront on the part of Manipur which had been subject to tribute until then which results in a punitive expedition by the Burmese which penetrates as far as Indian Bengal. This is a sensitive blow to the interests of the British East India Company – 1823 the first shots are fired in the first Anglo-Burmese war which ends three years later – after two annihilating defeats – in the Treaty of Yandabo; Assam, Tenasserim, Arakan and the border along Manipur fall into British hands. Flank protection – the original British aim – on the Gulf of Bengal is assured.

As far as England was concerned Burma had already been in the past a major trading partner; there had been contact with the Royal House of Taungu in Ava since 1687. The rich teak forests plus the function as through road for trade with China, had brought a speculative gleam to the eye of the lion in Brittania's colours. When the war breaks out with France too, the main competitor beyond India, the intention is to beat the opponent to the draw in this area too; securing flanks on the Gulf of Bengal is the chief aim of this military sandbox game. Burma however is the victim. The Birmans, wildly overestimating their military strength once more, bait the lion. Tharrawaddy followed his elder brother on the throne and had nothing better to do than break the treaty of 1826 as quickly as possible; Pagan Min, king since 1846, pushes events to a crisis; as was usual under his predecessors; he stages a massacre among potential heirs to the throne, with the exception that this time the cruel game takes place under the eyes of the British envoy and merchants. When finally, in 1852, two English captains complain of unfair treatment by a Burmese law court, the lion's next blow follows, and heralds the second Anglo-Burmese war (1852–1853), at the end of which Lower Burma is occupied and the first Governor appointed, Major Arthur

Phayne. Burma is becoming smaller and smaller.

That the current state of affairs cannot be allowed to continue is abundantly clear to the mighty of the Konbaung Dynasty. After a palace revolt against Pagan Min in 1853, Mindon Min takes over – in the sàme year – the reins of power. Reforms, a just system of taxation and waiver of customs taxes for the British Empire are intended to ease confrontation. Subjects travel to Europe to study, the administration is reformed and the first tentative steps towards industrialisation are made. Burma on the way to getting into line... which is not to bring the hoped for results. Mindon, a faithful Buddhist, transfers the capital from Amarapura to Mandalay (1861) on the 2,400th anniversary of Buddha's death, the swan song of the dynastic order of the country.

A glorious finale: in 1872 some 2,400 Burmese monks celebrate the 5th Buddhistic council, the first for 2,000 years; innumerable stonemasons are at work inscribing the holy canons (Tripitaka script of Buddhism) on 729 marble slabs. A white painted pagoda, which captures all the fabulous magic of Mandalay, is built over this "book of stone". Six years later Mindon Min dies in the belief he has left to his successor a well ordered nation rooted in the principles of Buddhism.

A belief on shaky foundations: Thibaw, his son and heir, executes his brothers and close relatives when he ascends the golden throne; Frenchmen are to be given a shipping agreement for the Irrawaddy, receive rights to travel via Bhamo to Chinese Yunnan; The British "Burma Trading Company" is sentenced to payment of heavy fines; the French are to receive rights to the teak forests – too much for the British lion, who raises its paw for the third time; after the third Anglo-Burmese war (1885–1886) the land has become a British colony. Thibaw and his ambitious wife find themselves in Indian exile. Pitiful interlude: the Burmese – Pyu, Mon and Birman – had established and administered great kingdoms; now they were administered as a province of British India. They were not even granted the status of a colony. Local revolts against the new masters brought little. Europeans, Chinese and Indians controlled a manner of trading based on western criteria and completely alien to the nature of the Buddhistic Burmese.

Dependency, also of an economic kind is the consequence. The deepest point is reached in 1919, from then on the way was to be up. In this year India is given partial autonomy with the "India Act". Burma on the other hand "remains before the door" in a manner of speaking, and is completely neglected. This has dire results; in 1920 there is the "December Strike" the first nationwide uprising against the colonial powers; great efforts are needed to extort the first reluctant concessions. Even greater events are in the air. Saya San is the name of the monk who, between 1930 and 1932, stirs up bloody revolt in the Tharrawaddy region; in spite of defeat, the spark spreads to Rangoon and ignites a powder keg which, in spite of the "Burma Act" (1935 the country becomes a colony with its own parliament), the colonial rulers are no longer able to extinguish. The elite of the student body organised in the "Young Men's Buddhist Association" after a tentative start in 1906, goes on strike and refuses to attend lectures at Rangoon University in 1936. Thakin – Master – the marxist trained leaders call themselves; two of them,

Thakin Aung San and Thakin U Nu, are to make history in only a few years. In 1937 they call for a boycott of elections under the colonial statutes.

"Aung San, you are the father of our nation" sing the Burmese children even today. They are right. When the leaders of the Thakin group are arrested by the colonial authorities in 1940, Aung San flees to Amoy and offers to collaborate with the Japanese; only one year later the army from the "Land of the Rising Sun" land in Lower Burma with the Burmese Liberation Army under Aung San. Among them U Nu and Ne Win, the subsequent leaders of Burma.

The jungle war on Burmese soil becomes an apocalypse for all concerned; there are 27,000 allied troops buried at Htaukkyan Cemetery near Rangoon alone. "Eat bitterness" and "the road of one man one mile" are only two of the phrases which put these jungle battles in the right blood soaked light. In December 1944 – after Burma had declared itself independent through the national government – Thakin Aung San takes up contact with the allies and changes sides with his renamed "Patriotic Burmese Forces" in March of 1945. A little later they march into Rangoon where, on the 28th of August, the Japanese capitulate. The merciless jungle warfare had brought innumerable dead, some heroes, and freedom for Burma…

For two years later, when it had become clear even in the backrooms of London's civil service, that Burma would never again permit itself to be forced into the status of colony, independence is an accepted fact. After receiving the agreement of the ethnic minorities, which Aung San had been able to win over in difficult negotiations at Panglong in Shan State, Prime Minister Attlee gives the green light; astrologers give the best date for independence as 4th January 1948.

National hero Aung San no longer sees this proud hour; on 19th June 1947 he is assassinated with 6 of his ministers. The 31 year old Thakin U Nu steps into his shoes and goes down in history as the first prime minister of Burma. And is confronted with almost insoluble economic and political tensions. Communist insurgents and Karen guerillas, fighting for their own state are at the gates of Rangoon. Civil war is only prevented by a hair. The German diplomat Rosiny: "The sweet fruits of freedom were already leaving a bitter taste". How true.

In spite of all the difficulties with which he is confronted U Nu is able to maintain his position until 1962; for two years (1958–1960) he places the rudder of state in the hands of the military and disappears behind Buddhist monastery walls. Bo Ne is the man of the hour, who, as general, sets numerous reforms in gear. As deus ex machina however U Nu returns to the Burmese political scene; with a demand for Buddhism as national religion. Surprisingly he wins the elections in February 1960, with the support of the AFPFL; this same AFPFL was founded by Aung San as the "Anti-fascist Peoples Freedom League" before independence was granted and in the meantime had risen to status of a major political party. But then the unity of the Burmese Union is at risk. U Nu not only wishes to institute Buddhism as national religion, he also appears receptive to efforts on the part of Mon, Arakanese, Shan and Kayah towards secession. Ne Win sees the danger; on March 2nd 1962 he gives the signal for the start of a powerful bloodless coup; U Nu goes into exile in Thailand (1968)

History at a Glance

Burma

Until 300 BC: Negritoes and the Malayan peoples leave almost no traces; the soil surrenders only a few stone artefacts.

From 300 BC to 1 AD: immigration of the Mon and Pyu; early Malayan peoples.

After 300 BC: Suvarnabhumi, the "Golden Land" of the Mon takes up relations with Ashoka's realms in India; centre Thaton in south Burma; Hinayana Buddhism in the first early stages.

300 to 500 AD: Sri Ksetra, Pyu state in Upper Burma is created.

8th to 10th centuries: Tibeto-Birmans reach Burma.

832: Pyu states Sri Ksetra and Halin destroyed by Thai and Shan tribes from the Thai realm Nan-Chao; end of the Pyu as a people.

Around the year 1000: Migration of the Burma peoples almost completed.

1044 to 1287: Pagan – first Birman Dynasty founded by Anawrahta (1044 to 1077) is conquered.

1057: Thaton, the Mon Hinayana Buddhism takes root.

1084 to 1167: Golden Age of Pagan under Kyanzittha and Alaung-sithu.

1287: Mongols conquer Pagan.

1287 to 1531: Shan rule in Upper Burma.

1287 to 1539: Wareru founds Mon realm in South Burma; chief cities Martaban and Pegu; renaissance of Hinayana Buddhism; last great realm of the Mon, which at the beginning of the 15th century is spread over great sections of what is present day Burma.

and thus gives both countries, after many years of separate history, once more an explosive point of contact with a time fuse. For once in Thailand U Nu builds up his so-called "freedom front" which according to him has 50,000 men under arms within only one year. The first armed clashes are won by Ne Win.

After the coup in 1962 a revolutionary council comprised of 17 officers conduct Burma's affairs of state for the next twelve years. In 1974 an elected

constitutional government takes over, and the "Socialist Republic of the Union of Burma" is born.

Unrest and a plan to topple the government, uncovered before it can be put into practice, make it known that Ne Win's government is not so undisputed after all.

Treading softly after 1980; after leaving the circle of non-aligned countries (1979), Ne Win strikes a conciliatory note which also includes amnesty for exiled politicians; U Nu returns to Ran-

1315: Establishment of Sagaing: independent Shan kingdom.

1364: Ava is established as the new capital of the Shan.

1519: First trading outpost of the Portuguese.

1531 to 1752: Taungu – second Birman dynasty founded by Tabinshwethi (1531–1550); Capital: Taungu, then Pegu and finally Ava.

1551 to 1581: King Bayinnaung as great conquerer: North Siam (Lan-na), Manipur, Luang Prabang and Ayutthaya. This regent of the Taungu Dynasty created Burma's present borders.

1613: Felip de Brito, for 13 years king of Syriam (Lower Burma), a Portuguese, is impaled.

1622 to 1638: the Arakan realm is at the peak of its powers under Thirithu-dhamma.

1635: New Taungu capital becomes the isolated Ava.

17th century: The British, French and Dutch gain power and establish outposts.

1747 to 1752: Mon rebellion, at the end of which Ava is conquered by the Mon king, Binnya Dala, who has himself crowned king at Pegu. Fall of the Taungu Dynasty.

1752 to 1885: Konbaung – third Birman dynasty. Founder: Alaungpaya (1752–1760); chief cities, Shwebo, Ava, Amarapura, Mandalay.

1760: Alaungpaya drives the Mon from Ava and becomes the founder of Rangoon (Yangon = end of the war).

1767: Conquer of Ayutthaya.
– 1784: Conquer of Arakan.

1824 to 1826: 1st Anglo-Burmese war; Treaty of Yandabo, the British occupy Tenasserim and Arakan.

1852/53: 2nd Anglo-Burmese war; British occupy Lower Burma. Major Arthur Phayre becomes first Governor.

1861: Mandalay is named capital of the Konbaung Dynasty.

goon and translates Buddhistic scriptures until his death. It comes as a complete surprise when Ne Win announces his resignation in 1981, without however surrendering chairmanship of the BSPP (Burma Socialist Program Party, founded in 1974 as a government party). U San Yu is appointed new president of Burma.

Some 1,500 years ago people in Thailand and Burma established the first kingdoms; on numerous occasions borders overlapped those of today; powerful kingdoms fought for dominance from the 12th century – changing destinies under changing dynasties; the thousand year old dynastic order was extinguished in Burma and Thailand at almost the same time in history. Military leaders took over power in strong hands; it is estimated that 30% of the population and 50% of the country are controlled by rebels today. The situation is probably similar in Thailand.

Many similarities – accord however with many dissonances.

1872: 5th Buddhistic Council in Mandalay. Birman culture is flourishing.

1885 to 1886: 3rd Anglo-Burmese war; Burma loses independence and becomes a province of the crown colony India. King Thibaw is banished to India.

1920: "December Strike" – a countrywide rising against the colonial powers organised by students.

1923: Dyarchy Reforms, partial self-government on the Indian pattern.

1930 to 1936: Founding of the Thakin union and university strike in Rangoon led by Thakin Aung San and Thakin U Nu.

1930 to 1932: Saya San uprising, which is brutally quashed.

1935: "Burma Act" separates Burma and India.

1937: Colonial status with own legislative powers.

1941 to 1945: Burma under Japanese occupation: severe jungle warfare.

1943: First declaration of independence by the Japanese puppet state.

1947: Attlee and Aung San negotiate independence.

19th July 1947: Aung San is assassinated.

4th January 1948: Burma becomes independent under premier U Nu.

1954 to 1956: 6th Buddhistic Council in Rangoon.

1958 to 1960: Military government under General Ne Win.

1960: New elections with surprise win for U Nu.

1962: Coup led by Ne Win and proclamation of the "Burmese Way to Socialism"; revolutionary council led by the military.

1974: New constitution and proclamation of "Socialist Republic the Union of Burma".

1975: Earthquakes destroy Pagan, numerous pagodas in ruins.

1979: Burma leaves the circle of non-aligned states.

1981: Ne Win resigns, remains chairman of his party; U San Yu new president.

Thailand

Around 10,000 BC: Archaeological finds in "Spirit Caves" of north Thailand include stone tools and prove that Thailand was settled then by agricultural peoples.

Around 3,500 BC: further archaeological finds prove once more the presence of the Negrito primeval inhabitants.

From around 300 BC to 1 AD the Mon immigrate, and with them the Khmer, who settle in Kampuchea (Cambodia); Karen peoples choose the isthmus of Siam for settlement. Transition from the Stone to Iron Age, Animism, mountains as sacred places for worshiping the gods. Assimilation of the primeval people; the first cultural influences from China and India. The Indian Emperor Ashoka sends Buddhistic monks.

200 AD: Funan kingdom with centre in the Mekong Delta also includes Thailand; first great realms beyond India with strong Indian influences.

600 AD: Probably under the rule of Funan, the Mon vassal state of Dvaravati is established with Lophuri as main city; at the end of the 9th century comes under Khmer rule. Dvaravati becomes the centre of Hinayana Buddhism beyond India.

800 AD: Foundation of the Mon kingdom Haripunjaya in the north of Thailand, which is conquered in the 13th century by the Thai ruler Mang Rai.

8th to 13th centuries: Immigration of the Thai from south China. The Thai a people of Mongolian origin, with much in common linguistically with the Chinese, had immigrated into West Yunnan in the 1st century AD; around 650 AD the kingdom of Nan-chao is founded, which is subjected to the Tang Dynasty in the 9th century and destroyed by Kublai Khan in 1253. Increased emigration to Thailand. During the same period south Thailand is under the control of the Sri Vijaya kingdom probably originating from Sumatra.

1238 to 1349: With Sukhothai there comes into existence under Ram Khamheng (approx. 1280 to 1317) as the most capable ruler, the greatest Thai kingdom in Thailand. The first major cultural era and development of the Thai alphabet. Sukhothai was founded by Indrapatindraditya.

1262: The Chiang Saen kingdom is founded in north Thailand by the Laotian prince Mang Rai; concentration takes place rapidly around Chiang Rai; in 1296 Chiang Mai becomes the new capital. Mang Rai allies himself to the prince of Phayo and Ram Khamheng and thus creates the kingdom of Lan-na; this exists until 1556 when it is destroyed by the Burmese Taungu ruler, Bayinnaung.

1349 to 1767: Thailand's Golden Age with the kingdom of Ayutthaya. Thibodi I (1350 to 1369) becomes, as the founder of this kingdom, the first ruler of all Thailand with the exception of Lan-na in the north.

1431: Conquer of Angkor and destruction of the Khmer realms.

1448 to 1488: Regency of King Boromo Trailokanat – deification of the ruler as Bodhisattva with the title "Holy Buddha"

1480: Conquest of border areas with Burma.

1569: The Burmese conquer Ayutthaya. King Naresuen (1574 to 1605) shakes off Burmese rule.

1594: Naresuen wins the duel with the Burmese Crown Prince and integrates Martaban into his realms between 1594 and 1614. First appearance of Europeans.

1657 to 1688: Under the rule of King Narai, art and culture reach peaks of perfection hitherto unknown; the Greek adventurer Constantine Phaukon acquires a private position of power as premier and is later assassinated. After Narais' death Siam closes its borders to the outside world. During this period Siam is considered the greatest power in South-east Asia.

1767: The Burmese Konbaung king, Ssinbyushin, destroys Ayutthaya.

1770: Paya Taksin establishes the new kingdom of Thonburi and wins back the territories occupied by the Burmese.

1782: Taksin, who in the meantime has become a megalomaniac, is assassinated. General Chakri ascends the throne of Siam as Rama I; Bangkok becomes the capital, several Burmese attacks are fended off.

1809: Phra Buddha, Loet La Naphalai, becomes new regent as Rama II. Tentative approaches are made to the British on the Malayan peninsula.

1824: Phra Nang Klao becomes Rama III. Victory over Vientiane in 1828. Supremacy over Vietnam is shared with Cambodia. Protestant missionaries enter the country, first tentative trading treaties with Europe.

1851: Rama IV Mongkut takes the throne. Trade treaties with 14 European powers, the Siam policy of isolationism is at an end. Mongkut becomes famous in Europe as a result of the novel "Anna and the King of Siam" (The King and I).

1868: The great reformer Chulalongkorn (or Phra Chula Chom Klao) becomes ruler of Siam as Rama V. Abolishment of slavery. Construction of transportation systems, change in educational methods. He visits Europe the first Siamese ruler to do so.

1910: Rama VI Vijiravudh ascends the throne. Educated at Oxford he serves in the British army; in World War I he supports the allies.

1925: King Prajadhipok, Rama VII, comes to power. During his reign in

1932: There is the coup which makes Siam a constitutional monarchy.

1935: Rama VII abdicates in favour of his nephew, educated in Switzerland. The new regent, Ananda Mahidol Rama VIII, transfers power to a "Royal Council" and remains in Switzerland.

1939: the country's name is changed to Thailand.

1941 to 1945: Thailand is used as a jumping off point by Japanese troops pushing towards Burma and Malaya: receives as compensation parts of Cambodia and Laos: at the end of the war a change to the allied front.

1946: Rama VIII is found shot and Rama IX Bhumipol is new king.

1955: Thailand joins SEATO.

1973: Violent student revolts in Bangkok, a new constitution is drawn up, 40 political parties come into being.

1977: Military government once more, and stricter.

1980: Bloodless change of government. General Prem Tinsulanonda becomes head of government. Since 1932 a total of 8 successful coups, the constitution is changed 9 times and set aside again just as frequently.

Focus on the Economy

Rice, rice and still more rice. This applies to the economies of both Burma and Thailand. Sober statistics are the best proof of this; 80% of all Thais earn their living in some way or other related to rice production, processing or sale; in spite of a downward trend Burma managed to reach a figure of 60% of all exports with rice, until 1962 the country was the worldwide leader in rice exports. Around 70% of the arable land in Thailand is reserved for the cultivation of rice; and that is some 16% of the total area of the whole country. Burma pumps 1 million tonnes annually onto the world's markets, although in the past this figure was nearer 3 million.

This is the broad outline; **agriculture** is the mainstay of the economies of both countries. But, the reverse side of the coin is, it is also unproductive. Around two third of all Thais, in Burma the figure is somewhat higher, are employed in some type of agricultural pursuit, but they account for only a meagre 30% of national income.

This has its reasons. On the delta around Bangkok, one of the traditional rice baskets of the land, around 90% of the fields are rented; and in the fruitful North and North-east, only half of the fields cultivated are owned by those who work them. The rents are very high and swallow some half of total yield, in spite of the fact that the powers that be in Bangkok stipulate that landowners are not entitled to a tithe of more than one quarter. Then there is the fact that the average farm with 2.4 hectares (some 5.9 acres) lies clearly below the minimum which permits a yield beyond that of the farmer's own needs. Agriculture in Burma opens up other, although by no means better, perspectives: even when there have been some modest successes with reforms in recent times, British colonial interests and various clumsy attempts at nationalisation on the part of the respective governments, often enough half-hearted and without taking the real needs of the people into account, have thoroughly disrupted a system of agriculture which existed, and worked, for centuries.

First it was the British who lauded officialdom and principles of economic performance as the patent for growth, which was contrary to the Buddhistic, and thus materially undemanding, nature of the Birmans. Then along came U Nu; he nationalised and collectivised because ownership of landed property had spread during British rule. When Ne Win took over in 1958 for two years it appeared that the rigid system instituted by U Nu relaxed, however U Nu returned to power and took up where he had left off; discouraging all foreign investors, state monopolies for all exports and imports.

When General Ne Win took over political leadership once more after a bloodless coup, the next breakdown was predestined in agricultural development; he not only pursued U Nu's policies further, he sharpened them considerably. For now all banks, major industries and the rice trade plus processing, were nationalised.

After rapid economic decline it was recognised only now that restrictions had been too tight and a careful start was made on relaxation of controls. Spare parts, imported fertilizers and pesticides assisted the agricultural "Trade Corporation", founded earlier, to operate more economically.

In Rank and File

Equally important to Thailand and Burma – rice. Basic commodity "the daily bread", without this, undisputed vital grain, Thailand and Burma would have to join the ranks of those countries where scarcity and hunger are the rule.

Rain, not always appreciated in other places, is here the very water of life; the water level in the rivers is just as important for irrigating the fields as is the rainfall for the growth of dry rice (7% of total land under cultivation is planted with rice). If the monsoon rains are meagre then an economic disaster, at very least, is certain. Rice exports fill the almost empty treasuries of Bangkok and Rangoon and excess production can still be sold easily abroad.

Rice farmers don't have an easy life, working as they do for the most part up to their knees in water; sowing, transplanting and harvesting demands sheer hard labour, mostly carried out in back-breaking manual work. Machines already in use in the United States are almost unknown. Some 1,000 hours of work per hectare (2.47 US acres) is calculated as required from sowing to threshing but even if a change took place in the low standard of living of the farmers this would not necessarily mean improved yield, for what is required is rationalisation and that is only possible with modern machines, which are beyond the reach of the small tenant farmer in Thailand and the co-operatives in Burma, alike.

Three types of cultivation are possible; dry or mountain rice planted in rain-fields and considered the tastiest as well as richest in vitamins and minerals; wet rice in natural flood areas or fields with artificial irrigation. The latter brings higher yields and when in the sixties American experts carried out tests with new hybridisation near Manila, good results were obtained very quickly; IR 8 is the name of the new "wonder rice" with larger grains only needing

Hope in the South is the term found by the Thais to describe the increased production of rubber on the Malayan peninsula, even when raw rubber was pushed to third place on the export hit list by maize. In Burma on the other hand rubber occupied, and still does, only a minor position.

Around 80 years ago (1901), the hevea plant which flourishes as a tree after some 5 years, and supplies raw rubber for 20 to 25 years, was brought by a far sighted governor to the southern Thai province from what was then British Malaya. Today the cultivated area covers some 3,500 square kilometres (around 1,352 square miles). Exports account for 10% of world needs. Thailand has thus pushed its way up to third place in the international ranks of producers behind Malaysia and Indonesia. Three million people, many of them Moslems, are engaged in winning latex. In the town of Haad Yai, in the south of Thailand, a Rubber Research Centre

four months for growth and which has been planted, mainly in Thailand with great success over the last decade. Disadvantages are increased use of artificial fertilizers and more susceptibility to pests, construction of new, more expensive, irrigation systems in order to improve control of water volume corresponding with plant growth.

Two fields are needed for cultivation. Special care is devoted to the seedbeds, which are in most cases, close to the house. In these the apple green shoots flourish until they range some 20 cm (8") above water level, watering takes place for the first time, very carefully, three days after sowing; scarecrows and woven mats protect the small beds.

After some 5 weeks the young plants are transplanted to the actual rice field, where frequently strings are drawn taut over the soil to make sure that the plants are really in "rank and file"; for only in this way can the rice flourish as it should. The field had already been ploughed immediately after the last harvest with stalks ploughed in as natural fertilizer; after saturating the earth the farmer levels the soil. Then it lies fallow for a few weeks before the shoots are planted out, after watering once more.

The plants change colour depending on the degree of ripeness, from pale green to yellowish green just before harvesting. Rice plants are cut off at the stalks just above the surface of the water and in many cases threshed alongside the field; and just as often tied in sheaves and transported to threshing mills.

Since rice grains remain in the ears even after threshing they have to be polished, and there are in Thailand alone some 25,000 mills, most owned by Chinese. A leader in exports, the "Thai Rice Company" has thought up something special; it markets vitamin enriched rice whereby so-called premix grains enriched 200 fold with vitamins and minerals are added in a ratio of 1 premix grain to 200 polished grains, and the enrichment is released during cooking.

is engaged in solving the question as to how national yield can be increased still further; at present this lies at around half of that of Malaysia, but whilst there plantations are the main sources, in Thailand something like 300,000 small operators have a hand in the pot; and they are answerable for 90% of total yield.

Natural rubber has the advantage of being unaffected by seasons and harvestable all year round. Each tree gives an average of 80 kg (176 lbs) latex annually. At four in the morning the workers start tapping the trees with spiral gashes in the bark which form a collecting ridge and a small cup is hung at the end. Two to three hours later the cups are collected and the latex brought to a provisional processing plant where it is cleaned and pressed into thin slabs before being transported to the rubber works. A skilled worker can tap up to 200 trees in just two hours.

Maize is a young grain in both Thailand and Burma only really known for three decades. In good places it can be harvested twice a year, otherwise it is planted alternately with rice. The so-called maize belt of Thailand between Lopuri and Chiangmai supplies 90% of national yield alone. As far as exports are concerned maize has taken over the position previously held by sugar, and has become the second most important export after rice. Neighbouring countries in East and South-east Asia are the main customers.

Starch from Manioc. This tuber of the spurge family with a starch content of 15% to 22% per root is vital to starch production and the nutrition of the people. Exports of the roots, crushed and dried in the sun, are mainly to Holland. Harvesting is done manually; 6 to 9 months after planting – other types take longer, some as much as four years – the bushes, many the height of a full grown male, are pulled, plus roots, out of the soil; harvesting machines still haven't become popular here.

For 100 years now the forests and jungles of Thailand and Burma have been plundered, felling without reafforestation was the maxim for quick profits. That **forestry** is today, in both countries, still a major economic factor, is due exclusively to natural wealth.

Teak, Yang and Andamanic redwood as well as ironwood occasionally contribute to easing the chronically empty state purses of Bangkok and Rangoon. These fine woods are almost exclusively intended for export; one welcome side effect is that the Yang delivers oil for production of lacquer. Without doubt the leader among the timber, is now as in the past, teak, which is felled in Burma's Shan Highlands and in Thailand's Northern provinces. Burmese teak is considered the best in the world, with American and German furniture makers as major customers. Laws recently introduced forbid felling of teak without official permission.

Bamboo, rattan, kenaf and sisal are primarily only significant locally for making sacking and ropes and the furniture industry.

Specialists describe the wealth that slumbers under the soil of Thailand and Burma as undisturbed treasure houses. And the forecast is that winning of **natural resources** promises well for the future, particularly in Burma. Oil found at the central Irrawaddy and trial drilling in the Gulf of Martaban and off the Arakan coast paint an optimistic picture of future independence from outside energy supplies with vast savings in precious, and scarce, foreign currency.

Cobalt, nickel, gold, copper, zinc and tin are all bounties of nature said to be available in amounts which warrant mining. But what is a present day reality: precious stones – officially sales are under Burmese government control – leave the country via smugglers' routes for Thailand; near Mogok in the Northern Shan state, valuable rubies and sapphires are mined; their unmistakable mark of quality is the starlike reflection of light. The Kachin State brings forth that wonderful apple green jade which fetches the highest prices on international markets and Burma the reputation of being the supplier of the highest quality jade.

By far the most valuable mineral in Thailand on the other hand is tin ore. In the areas around the Malayan Peninsula, which are Thai territories, the Chinese had for centuries mined the metal.

Thailand is, after Malaysia and Bolivia, the world's third largest producer of tin. Supplying mainly to the United States and Japan. Apart from tin only tungsten is mined in any considerable amount. Thailand has however several deposits of precious stones where rubies and sapphires are won at depths of up to 10 metres (33 ft). Cutting and polishing is carried out for the most part by small family businesses in Bangkok.

Fish is, after rice, the staple food for the people of both countries. **Fishing** is therefore a major economic factor, and for this reason the Institute of Marine Biology was founded, with German aid, in 1965 in Bangkok which three years later also included a school of fishery.

Nevertheless Thai waters, especially inland, would appear to be overfished. A 390 square kilometres (around 140 square miles) area of marshlands near Nakhon Sawan was transformed under a government scheme into a lake which is to serve as new breeding grounds for fish. At present some 1.5 million tons of sea and freshwater fish flounder in Thai nets; and this amount could increase in the near future. Fishing is being determinedly pursued in the waters of the Gulf of Thailand, the Indian Ocean and the South China Seas, the possibility of preserving and utilising waste products is however still in its infancy.

Burma's "Martaban Fishing Company" called into life with Japanese aid, operates with its fleet off the coast of Tenasserim. The main source of protein is still however fish caught in inland waters.

Both countries are still backward as far as development of **industry** is concerned. Burma is still limping far behind Thailand in this respect. Industrialisation only took place in Thailand fifty years ago; when in the thirties, British trade privileges in Thailand were finally undermined, the fragile plant of industrialisation took root. Today around 50,000, mainly small industrial undertakings, employ some 8% of the working population. And to be taken into account here is the fact that the 25,000 rice mills in the country have also been included in this figure. The few large companies produce iron and steel, cement, artificial fertilizers, crude oil products, tobacco, cotton, paper and textiles; production of electronic equipment is being developed. Concentration of the companies in and around Bangkok, taken in conjunction with neglect of other parts of the country, has had a negative effect. Only 12% of national income comes from industry, whereas around 20% stems from the more efficiently organised service fields.

Eighteen out of every 100 gainfully employed persons in Burma earn a living in industry. According to official economic policies expansion of small and medium sized businesses is to be furthered before more industrialistion takes place. In terms of value, around half of all industrial production is devoted to foodstuffs, beverages and tobacco, followed by edible oils, fish canning, cotton textiles and processing crude oil, iron and steel products. Industrial centre is Rangoon, with Mandalay – still lagging some way behind – up and coming in industrial development (textiles, beverages).

Keep your feet on the Ground – Take to the Air: Transport

Keeping your feet on the ground is no problem at all in Thailand – if you don't number among those tourists for whom a three day visit is already one day too long. The Thai system of roadways is first class judged by Asiatic standards; public buses connect all rural areas not only with Bangkok, but also each other. And if you need the last word in comfort, clamber into one of the latest type air-conditioned buses.

All weather roads – if you discount the strategically important connections between Bangkok and the North, financed with US dollars – spread throughout the land. And a rented car is no problem either, major road junctions and place names are on all road signs in Latin letters with the exact number of miles. Prices are low at least compared with those in Europe. But you have to have a tendency towards the left – as far as traffic is concerned naturally. You drive on the left.

If you should hire a taxi the iron rule is – haggle! Otherwise you won't only be, unnecessarily, a few Baht poorer, you'll also be seen by the natives as a squanderer. The rule of thumb is; before getting in offer half of the fare asked and then meet halfway; the driver still earns well – and you are seen with new eyes as a well seasoned traveller to be taken seriously.

The same applies by the way to the Samlors – smelly, noisy, three-wheeled conveyances mainly found in Bangkok – to the horse drawn carriages and the bicycle rickshaws, these latter are only found in certain places; you can travel all over the city at a fairly reasonable price. It just takes somewhat longer.

And if you can't do without the calming rattle of trains even on holiday, then Thailand has quite a lot to offer. Via the railroad, stretching out like an octopus from Bangkok, you can reach even the remotest parts of the country; Chiang Mai is on the timetable, as is Nong Khai on the Laotian border and Nam Tok in the West on the River Kwai, or Butterworth in Malaysia (with connections to Singapore); those sensitive to heat should pay the extra charge for air conditioned coaches, and a couchette is advisable on night trips. German engineers had quite a lot to do with the development of the Thai railroad. Water and air on the other hand have no sleepers. The Thai national airline serves 22 destinations at prices which are justified by first class service. The "air hop" from Chiangmai back to Bangkok – if you have travelled out by car, bus or rail – takes one hour. And saves travelling through countryside you've seen already anyway. For those who just can't wait, there is even a "Pattaya Service" on Fridays and Sundays, a 15 minute flight to the beaches; by car even the most daring Thai driver needs two hours!

Hardly recommended on the other hand are the shipping services from various ports to other countries or another Thai port. Equipment and standards are South-east Asiatic, and accidents fairly frequent accordingly. As a tourist the only services worth considering are the ferries from coastal towns to beaches, but it should be kept in mind that even on these short trips the waves are such as can put even the best sea-legs to a severe test.

And in the West – still quiet – Burma restricts visitors to stays of 7 days only. Groups can, under certain conditions, stay one day longer. This tight time limit makes air travel almost the only ideal means of conveyance. But; a word of warning, all too much faith placed in published schedules verges on blue-eyed innocence, almost childlike trust. The few, often aged – and accordingly rattling, machines (with the exception of the sensational purchase of three new generation "Fokkers") appear to operate on the basis of co-operation rather than a schedule. Western traffic managers would tear their hair!

More by luck than intent, everything turns out alright in the end. Burmese are past masters in the art of improvisation; Pagan, Mandalay, Heho and back to Rangoon, and of course in the other direction too, is the tourist "rat race" of the "Golden Triangle" for a one week stay; all done by air – because of the time factor – see above. Lately the resort of Sandoway on the Gulf of Bengal has been included in tourist itineraries with daily flights, and Moulmein too, although permission isn't always granted.

Reservations have to be made for overland trips well in advance and single tourists are not always given permission to untertake these. The political situation and lack of facilities (no hotels etc.), in many parts of the country, are responsible. Under certain organisational exceptions (lack of seats on aircraft for example) the road from Lower to Upper Burma is open to foreigners but only via a bumpy bus. Taxis can of course be found in the larger Burmese towns, but bargaining is out in this socialist country. A full hour costs 20 Kyatt at present and is used in Rangoon as a minimum for calculating the final fare which is always higher. Horse carriages (in Mandalay) are somewhat cheaper, and maybe safer too than the bone-shaking pre-war cars.

The Burmese railway bears the unmistakable stamp of the British lion (4,000 kilometres = approx. 2,480 miles) and is used by tourists mainly on the routes Rangoon to Mandalay or Rangoon – Thazi (and from there on by road to Pagan). Trains are surprisingly comfortable (adjustable seats), so that the day's travel from Madalay back to Rangoon with the colourful activity at the wayside stations provides many rewarding impressions. Other connections from Rangoon are to Prome, Martaban, Pyinmana.

An absolute must, if time permits, is a trip on the Irrawaddy. Specially praiseworthy is the trip from Mandalay to Pagan with several stops at untouched villages which can be used for sightseeing – much too briefly – (completely unspoiled rural life); the trip takes between 10 to 24 hours depending on whether the ship has been chartered for a group of tourists or is on its "normal run". Always subject of course to there being no sandbanks to turn the already very rough timetable completely upside down. (The trip in the other direction is not recommended, it takes too long). There are also shorter Irrawaddy trips to, among other places, Mingun starting from Mandalay.

Something for all Tastes – Hotels, Tourism

Everyone visiting Bangkok simply has to go there at least once, even if only for a drink at the poolside or one of the bars; "Oriental" is the name of that most distinguished, most elegant hotel with the most tourist comforts. Plus the fact that the hotel on the banks of the Chao Phaya (Menam) wallows in tradition, which is skillfully marketed. Many famous people – the only word for it, one just doesn't "stay" at a hotel of this kind – resided here, among others Somerset Maugham. And through their presence raised the luxurious surroundings beyond that of merely an hotel. Whilst in the old part memories of yesteryear are conjured up, the German manager runs the modern "Oriental" with all its luxury, with a quiet perfection which brought him the title of "Manager of the Year" in 1982.

But there are other hotels in Bangkok, apart from the "Oriental", available in the luxury class and comparatively more reasonably priced; between 26 to 42 US dollars per night and room, with lots of comfort. There is also still more reasonably priced accommodation for those who have to be a little more careful with the pennies, or the more price conscious, ranging from around 6 US dollars to just over 15 US dollars. These too offer adequate comforts and sometimes even several restaurants plus swimming pool. First class, genuinely luxurious quarters are found outside Bangkok primarily at Chiang Mai.

The same applies to this second most popular tourist resort as to the metropole; the total number of hotels is lower, but so are prices too. And at the beach resorts (mainly Pattaya or Cha-am) accommodation can be found ranging from simple to extravagant depending on taste and pocket.

The "Royal Cliff" at Pattaya occupies a special position in the same way as the "Oriental" at Bangkok. New hotels, such as are found at Kamphaengphet, or complete modernisation (the best example is the "Wiang Inn" at Chiangrai) have raised hotel standards considerably in recent times in other parts of Thailand. But even today the provinces have remained just that – provincial, as far as hotel quality is concerned. At Lopburi for instance, which every Thai tourist in search of culture would visit, the "Asia" numbers among the best; at this simple hotel, where rooms are rented on an hourly basis too, the meals are just about the only consolation for general dreariness.

Thailand still ranks first in tourist popularity, alongside Sri Lanka (Ceylon), even after many years at top of the list; a tourist attraction which draws more than one million foreigners yearly and whose appeal would appear to be undimmed. Heavenly beaches, impressive pagodas and monasteries, wonderful landscapes, reasonable prices, and last, but by no means least, the Thais themselves – with their warm friendliness and hospitality – ensure that the star of Thailand will burn bright in the tourists dream of paradise. A relatively minor drop in visitors in 1981 had been made good again only one year later.

Another tourist draw is Burma. Much less western oriented than Thailand, this fairytale country of Southeast Asia ranks high in the favour of experienced globetrotters. And fairytale in the sense used here means fabulously beautiful. The stranger sees an Asia here in the process of applying the first touches of the make-up of western civilisation, 20th century style. The restrictive policies of the central government in Rangoon is, with grants of stay of only up to 7 days, in one way regrettable, but also understandable in view of the lack of tourist facilities (too few hotels, etc.), plus the fact that rebellious tribes in many parts of the country create areas which have to be left off the tourist maps.

Originality is the feature that sells Burma. This same originality however also applies to hotels, and that luxurious sparkle, which is offered the tourist, at least at the main resorts in Thailand, is searched for in vain in Burma.

Until now hotel building was a long way down the list of government priorities; there has been, it is true, a change in this attitude, at least a few tentative steps, but this hasn't relieved the hotel situation all that much, not enough anyway to make a noticeable difference. A lot of water will have to flow down the Irrawaddy before the government can put those projects, prematurely announced, into practice; at the main tourist centres, new, high standard hotels are planned to overcome the bottleneck.

For the present the tourist has to accept what's offered. And that is very little. The "Inya Lake Hotel" is considered the best address in Rangoon, but it still does not match up to even mere average accommodation in Bangkok.

The good old "Strand" has even deteriorated to second class, even when teak panelled rooms, and in particular the dining room, stir up memories of better days. Burma's pride remains beyond all shadow of a doubt the "Thiripyitsaya" at Pagan. Bungalows decorated in local style on the banks of the Irrawaddy, a main building – that also earns the name – a bar and an appealing restaurant, raise the "Thiripyitsaya" to the level of national flagship. The only drawback; demand exceeds availability many times over. Rooms are hard to get, above all during the peak season November to February.

At Mandalay and Inle Lake, the two other most popular destinations for tourists, the situation is even worse. Whilst the "Mandalay Hotel", an unimaginative heap of stone can only, even with the best of will, be compared with a 3rd class railway waiting room, the hotel at Taunggyi ("Strand") still breathes some of the atmosphere of colonial times as what is left of a onetime popular British "hill station", and the gardens in front are really pretty. Those in the know equip themselves with a warm sweater or light coat for the cool evenings and nights.

There are plans now for building a new hotel ("Mya Mandalay Hotel") in the near future, which should help some.

Only one relatively good hotel at Sandoway, and only one, really simple, at each of the resorts Kalaw, Pegu and Moulmein, plus another in a somewhat better class at Maymyo, completes the scanty offer. But as already mentioned, a lot of water will have to flow down the Irrawaddy before all the projects planned become reality; time in Burma is different from time in other places, mainly due to lack of finances.

If "Tourist Burma", the national tourist organisation with head office in Sule Pagoda Road, right next door to the ancient, venerable, pagoda, really had a say in matters, large sections of the country would long since have been developed for tourists and more hotels built. The pleas of these professionals, some trained in Europe, have fallen on deaf ears, at least until now, at the various ministries concerned. By the way if you travel individually to Burma, your first outing should be to "Tourist Burma". They will give you all the information you need, confirm flights, and make hotel reservations for places outside Rangoon; they also have locally trained guides available.

Burma really doesn't have to make much effort to appeal to tourists. The country is so fascinating that any lack of comfort becomes rapidly what in fact it really is; a slight inconvenience.

Some like it hot – Climate, the best time to travel

Thailand and Burma have much the same weather conditions, whereby it should be kept in mind that there are certain local differences. Rainfall and seasonal frequency are determined by the monsoons, which don't take place throughout the land at the same time. In principal; between the beginning of November and the end of February, is the best time for both countries. Whilst we, in Europe at least, are suffering the trials of Winter, the rainy season has come to an end in Thailand and Burma and daytime temperatures are relatively mild (Burma around 23°C / 73°F; Thailand 24°C / 75°F) which makes the stay pleasant for those from cooler climes.

Don't forget though; both countries are in the tropics and midday temperatures even during the "cool" season can climb to 30°C / 86°F, and over. Plus the fact that humidity, above all in the coastal regions, is high – in Bangkok 80% annual average – so that muggy, close, days are not rare in Winter in the countries beyond India, respectively in South-east Asia.

Thailand is completely at the mercy of the seasonal monsoons, but in Burma the mountains in the North are seen to be an additional weather break which prevent penetration of the cooler air masses from Central Asia.

From October to March the dry North-east monsoon dictates the climate of both countries. Temperatures reach their lowest levels in November and climb quickly towards the end of the dry season. Days with temperatures around 40°C (104°F) are frequent, mainly in low-lying areas and those at some distance from the coast.

There are three main seasons in Thailand:

1. Winter, from November to February, considered the best for tourists.

Climatic Table

Place	height above sea level (in m)	average air temperature in Centigrade/Fahrenheit			average yearly rainfall		
		Jan.	July	Aver.	in mm	Max.	Min.
Bangkok	12	26.0/79.0	28.5/83.0	28.0/82.0	1530	Sept.	Dec.
Chiang Mai	310	21.5/71.0	27.5/81.5	26.0/79.0	1325	Sept.	Dec.
Nakhon Sawan	28	25.0/77.0	29.0/84.0	28.0/82.0	1192	Sept.	Dec.
Udon Thani	174	22.5/73.0	28.5/83.0	27.0/81.0	1465	Sept.	Dec.
Songkla	10	26.5/80.0	28.0/82.0	27.5/81.5	2050	Nov.	Feb.
Rangoon	23	24.5/76.0	27.0/81.0	27.0/81.0	2550	Aug.	Dec.
Mandalay	76	20.0/68.0	29.5/85.0	27.0/81.0	750	May	Feb.
Moulmein	22	25.5/78.0	26.0/79.0	27.0/81.0	4565	Aug.	Jan.

Average annual temperatures:
Burma: 26°C/79°F
Thailand: 26°C/79°F

Best time for travel:
Burma: November – February
Thailand: November – February

Second best:
Burma: October and March/April
Thailand: March – May (high season at beach resorts)

Hottest seasons:
Burma: May (up to 41°C/106°F)
Thailand: May (up to 41°C/106°F)

Heaviest rainfall:
Burma: August/September
Thailand: September (90% of annual average rainfall in the rainy season between July and October

Footnote: the amount of rainfall varies considerably from place to place (see under Mandalay and Rangoon, plus Nakhon Sawan and Songkla); and even during the so-called rainy season it does not rain all the time in all places. During the relatively cool "Winter" (November – February) warmer clothing is needed for evenings (sweaters, light coats, for those places located higher above sea level such as Taunggyi/Burma or the North/North-east of Thailand, where temperatures can sink as low as 5°C/41°F.

The Tai peninsula Malakka is a climatic special case: the difference in temperatures between the coolest and warmest months is only 3°C/37°F. During the European summer months, rainfall is heaviest on the West coast (Phuket) and during the European Winter, on the East coast (Hua Hin), and there are no really clearly defined dry or rainy seasons.

Lifelines – the Rivers

River	length in km/miles (navigable in km/miles)	river basin in square km/ square miles
Irrawaddy	2,250/1,398 (1,500/932)	410,000/ 15,830
Salween	2,480/1,541 (150/ 32)	296,000/114,286
Sittang	450/ 280 (——)	40,000/ 15,444
Chao Phaya (Menam)	365/ 227 (350/217)	20,000/ 7,722 (delta only)
Nan	627/ 39 (——)	——*
Ping	590/ 367 (——)	——*
Chindwin	800/ 497 (180/112)	——**

* sources of the Chao Phaya (Menam)
** flows into the Irrawaddy

2. Summer, from March to May with high temperatures; even the natives flee to the beaches.

3. The rainy season from June to October; The South-west monsoon ensures generous rainfall, humidity is extremely high and hard to take by those from less extreme climates, in particular Europeans.

There are however possibilities of escape – the North and North-east of Thailand are not only several degrees cooler – on yearly average – there ist also less rain.

Almost the same applies to Burma, mainly to those places open to foreign tourists, except that in this case there are marked dry seasons inland, while on the coast up to six times more rain has been recorded.

Dragon and Elephant Head – The Nature of the Land

Dry facts on a dry land, at least in the shelter of the Arakan mountains (Mandalay Plains); the "Socialistic Republic of the Union of Burma", so the official name of the country, measures 687,033 square kilometres (265,263 sq. mi.). Between the 28th and 10th degrees of the northern latitude this biggest mainland country of South-east Asia stretches 2,000 kilometres (1,243 miles) in length, the largest East-West distance however is only 900 kilometres (559 miles) between the 92nd and 103rd degrees of latitude. The longest of its borders is shared with Thailand (1,600 kilometres / 994 miles), 1,520 kilometres (944 miles) bind it to the People's Republic of China, 1,040 kilometres (646 miles) with India and each 240 kilometres (149 miles) with Laos and Bangladesh; on the other side it is almost 2,000 kilometres (1,243 miles) of coastline – Andaman Sea, Gulf of Martaban and Gulf of Bengal – and natural chains of mountains which enclose the land against the outside world.

A little less dry; the imaginative see a dragon in the shape of the country, with the narrow estuary of the Tenasserim forming the tail, whereas the Irrawaddy is the long lifegiving line to which the dragon is bound.

The British called this major river symbolically "The Road to Mandalay". It rises in the southern Himalayas and carries from North to South along 2,170 kilometres (1,348 miles) (in all 2,250 kilometres / 1,398 miles) precious moisture; its nine armed Delta,

some 300 kilometres (186 miles) wide, embraces the rice basket of Burma, the most fruitful section of the country, before it pours its muddy waters into the Andaman Sea. From here ships are able to navigate 1,500 kilometres (932 miles) up the Irrawaddy to the interior as far as Bhamo in the Shan uplands, through the dry plains of Central Burma where the historic kingdoms of Sri Kastra and Pagan flourished on its banks. However, Pegu, 90 kilometres (56 miles) north of Rangoon was still in the 16th century the major port; the Elephant River (= Irrawaddy) is the cause of Pegu being so far from the sea today, the Delta is silting up at a rate of 50 metres (164 ft.) out to sea yearly. And provides additional arable land. With its tributary the Chindwin, it forms the major junction for the economy and shipping. "The Road to Mandalay" – the British were not entirely wrong, 409,000 square kilometres (157,915 sq. mi.), two third of total land area lie within the basin of this one river.

In addition to this lifeline there are two other rivers of major significance to the dragon of Burma, as far as irrigation and transport are concerned, the Chindwin and the Salween. Good 100 kilometres (62 miles) south of Mandalay the Irrawaddy enters the natural bed of the Chindwin, which above this point wanders through the Sagaing Province and the north-westerly part of the country; the Chindwin is navigable 180 kilometres (112 miles) towards the North before the rivers join. The Salween on the other hand gouges deep gorges into the Shan uplands before it reaches its destination 2,480 kilometres (1,541 miles) further on in the Gulf of Martaban near Moulmein. It can be navigated for only a short 150 kilometres (93 miles) upwards from the estuary before the deep gorges make it impassable; and it is alleged that at these points there are fluctuations in levels of up to 20 metres (66 ft.). But it is eminently suitable as a means of transport for fine timber felled in the Shan mountains (teak for instance).

Another great river in Burma has become old and tired, where once the Mon sowed the tender seeds of what was to become a flourishing culture at the mouth of the Sittang. It is silted to such an extent today that even boats with a very shallow draft can only navigate a short stretch.

Four types of landscape leave an unmistakable imprint on Burma; Western Birman mountains, Irrawaddy Basin, Irrawaddy Delta and finally the Shan uplands. A range of mountains 1,500 km (932 miles) long pushes its way from North to South as a barrier between the backlands of India and South Asia. It begins triumphantly in the North where it soars 5887 metres, in all its glaciated might as the highest point in South-east Asia close to the border of Tibet (Hkakabo Razi); the giants reduce in size in the Kachin Mountains, but still reach 3,000 metres (984 ft.), with rain forests in the tropical belt. This is the home of the Kachin, Lisu and Naga with their terraced fields.

As the Arakan Mountains, the range of mountains in the West of Burma assume the character of a secondary chain until finally they disappear into the sea at "Pagoda Point". The Peaks ranging out of the Andamans and Nicobars as well as the mighty mountains of North and West Sumatra, Java and the small Sunda Islands, are nothing more than a continuation of these Arakan Mountains and in other words an arm of the Himalayas pushing south.

The central flat lands are drained by the river system of the Irrawaddy. In the North the hilly country of the Gangaw, Kumon and Mingin Yoma and in the South those of Pegu Yoma, form natural divides between the Chindwin, Irrawaddy and Sittang. Marine and terrestrial sediment have filled these wide depressions between the Shan uplands and the Arakan Mountains, and marine sediment recovered at Pegu Yoma has been found to contain oil. The alluvial soil of the plains serves above all in the cultivation of rice. There is however also here volcanic activity along a so-called volcano line, in as far as local elevations are concerned, which stretches over the Mingin Yoma and the northern Pegu Yoma towards the Irrawaddy Delta; the 1,518 metres (4,980 ft.) high Andesite peak of Mount Popa is named as only one example here (refer to separate chapter). This Central Burma, or "Burma proper" as the British called it, was also the original settling place of the Birmans; and still today, true to colonial customs, is divided into Lower and Upper Burma. The dividing line runs somewhere around the middle between Rangoon and Mandalay near the towns of Prome and Taungu.

The giant Delta of the Irrawaddy, measuring some 300 by 300 km (186 by 186 miles), densely populated and the rice basket of the country, is of major importance. A mangrove coast closes off the wide spreading area from the sea.

The fourth and last natural contour of the country is the Shan uplands. It rises with a fracture zone of the central plains, is deeply furrowed and on average 1,000 metres (3,281 ft.) high, with mountains which in places reach a height of 2,500 metres (8,202 ft.). These highlands with an almost European climate, home of the Shan people, represent a natural continuation of the northern Kachin mountains, and continue towards Thailand and Laos. The most ancient rock formations in Burma – gneiss and granite – are found here. Potatoes, cotton, ground nuts, tobacco, coffee and opium are cultivated.

A natural border to Thailand is formed by the Tenassarim Range, the tail of the dragon, which spreads southwards. Really intensive agricultural cultivation anly takes place in the vicinity of Tavoi (original home of the Inle Lake Inthas), Moulmein and Mergui. The Mergui Archipelago jutting out from the Tenasserim is considered a completely unspoiled island idyll, which has however been claimed by the smugglers as their own.

From the dragon to the elephant. Land divisions in Thailand don't differ all too greatly from those of Burma. The change from the dragon to the elephant's head is not such a big change after all. There is one major difference in spite of this, the elephant's head is smaller. Thailand covers an area of 514,000 square kilometres (198,455 sq. mi.), about the size of France. From the extreme North to the deep South close to Malaysia the "Land of the Free" stretches more than 1,700 km (1,056 miles), the spread along the 15th parallel of latitude is 750 km (466 miles).

If the shape of Burma can be justifiably compared with a dragon, then the comparison of Thailand with an elephant's head, even more so. The drooping trunk is symbolised by the narrow Malakka Peninsula stretching towards the South; the Korat Plateau in the East is the ragged ear, the mountains of the North, the jutting bones of the forehead and Bangkok, at the south end of the central plains, represents the eye socket. And this at the same time illustrates all typical land formations.

From South to North: the Malayan Peninsula, which Thailand shares with Burma and Malaysia, hunches its mountainous spine, which provides a strict division in particular of the West coast. Off the island of Phuket, 820 km (510 miles) from Bangkok – and rich in tin – the spine disappears into the sea. However along the East coast flat basins have spread out offering an opportunity for rice cultivation and animal husbandry. And in addition, chemical weathering has created bizarre, rugged points in the crystalline slate and lime such as also attract much attention in the central plains of Thailand.

The mountain chain bordering India spreads towards the East in four massive ranges; the West Burmese boundary chain; South-east Asian central chain; Annam Mountains and the southern Chinese mountainous country. Of the three lower areas located among these mountains the western is incorporated into the central flatlands of Burma, and the middle by the central flatlands of the Thai Menam Basin. This plain stretching 500 km (311 miles) from the Gulf of Siam towards the North is the heart of Thailand. Monsoon rains transform the 30,000 square kilometres (11,583 sq. mi.) bed into a giant reservoir which irrigates innumerable acres of rice. The Chao Phaya flows through the plain and provides an ideal road for transportation of goods to Bangkok; it also carries arable soil from the mountains and is a major source of water for the rice fields of the South. In as far as fruitfulness is concerned the delta landscape, which annually spreads a further 6 metres (19'8") into the Gulf of Siam, compares favourably with the Irrawaddy Delta in Burma.

There is no flatter or more level region on earth than Bangkok, 30 km (18,6 miles) from the sea. It is said that the highest natural rise is no more than 2 metres (6'7"); 100 km (62 miles) away at Ayutthaya, it reaches double this, a proud 4 metres (13 ft.); and even at Nakhon Sawan, which is after all 250 km (155 miles) from the sea, only 24 metres (78'9") is measured. Tides can have effect as far as Ayutthaya from the Chao Phaya, which has almost no estuary, and floods simply can't be prevented in the flat areas, so that building on piles, so typical of Thailand, is truly justified.

The flatlands at both sides of the Chao Phaya are in all probability alluvial areas caused by masses of mud and soil brought down by great rivers; when trial drilling took place no solid rock was found even as far down as 400 metres (1,312 ft.). However at the edges of these plains gentle rolling hills, steep single mountains and even whole chains of mountains rise up. Something of special interest for photographers are the isolated pillars of lime, bizarre peaks in the plains, which are probably the remains of spurs of the backs of mountains which were formed by erosion of the rock (underground rivers).

East of the Thai rice bowl there is then the high plateau of Nakhon Ratchasima, the uplands of Korat. The 200 m (656 ft.) high plateau drops slightly towards the East and drains down to the Mekong which forms a long section of the border to Laos; Cambodia (Kampuchea) Laos, Burma and Malaysia are neighbouring countries, the Gulf of Siam and the Andaman Sea border Thailand towards the South China Seas and the Indian Ocean. In the south-west, where the 1,000 m (3,211 ft.) high southern and 700 m (2,297 ft.) high western edges of the Korat Plateau meet, Khao Laem ranges 1,328 metres (4,357 ft.). Extreme shortage of water during the dry season provides a really barren landscape compared with the lushness of the Menam plains. Large areas are open savannah where animal husbandry and the cultivation of maize, cotton and kenaf are the agricultural pursuits.

The South-east Asiatic central chain in the West and the Annam Mountains in the East determine the terrain of Thailand in the North and West. Statistics state that Doi Angka south of Chiang Mai is Thailand's highest mountain with 2,576 metres (8,451 ft.). Several chains of mountains run parallel to each other from the North in a southerly direction with wide valleys between; from here the five major tributaries run into the Chao Phaya (Pasak, Ping, Wang, Yom and Nan). The dark, jungle mountains – which do not lend themselves to human culture – frame attractive valleys where rice is planted. These mountains are however the home of several tribes who cultivate small fields by burning down the trees, and move on when the soil is spent. In this way a problem becomes obvious in the North which can't be overlooked even on the Korat Plateau – increasing waste land spread over large areas. Because of clearing by means of burning on the mountain sides, and rapid exhaustion of the soil through cultivation, the already thin tropical humus only provides Alan-alang grass or worthless secondary bushes. All ambitious schemes for reafforestation, some under the leadership of international experts, have been in vain. A dreary outlook; in a few years one third of Thailand's territory could be desert. An elephant's head, without hair.

Beautiful Cats –
The Animal World

She has won prizes at beauty competitions all over the world and led to admiration on the part of both male and female among Homo sapiens. Where she came from originally is still something of a mystery. Her name? Vichien Mas; we call her the Siamese cat. And with her blue eyes and cream coloured coat she really is a beauty.

Cats are a familiar sight in both Thailand and Burma and just as popular as house pets as they are here. This has gone so far that certain types, for instance the Thai Korat cat became a symbol for success and happiness, but in the same way as success and happiness, this cat is also rare in Thailand.

A great deal was attributed to her, and numerous legends surrounded the animal whose eyes change from pale blue to deep green with increasing age, with its blueish coat with the sheen of silver. Since this silvery sheen is similar to that of real silver – according to the Thais – ownership of a Korat cat was said to increase a merchant's hoard of silver and farmers with these cats hoped for especially good harvests because their eyes were the colour of young rice.

Less beautiful and appealing than the cats of Burma and Thailand are the snakes, which abound, ranging from the 6 metres (19'8") long, harmless, python to the less harmless krait, cobra and Russel viper. King cobras can reach a length of four metres (13'2") and more. Fear of poisonous snakes however is unfounded if one moves carefully in open country; to rush blindly through high grass on the other hand would be inviting trouble.

At the Bangkok Pasteur Institute, which belongs to the Thai Red Cross, fear of snakes also became a business, for it's here that a "Snake Farm" is kept where hundreds of snakes are held in three great pits for the production of serum. The reptiles are milked daily at 10 a. m. with a kind of casual ease which brings goose-pimples out on the watching tourists. The venom is injected into horses and their blood is used to make the serum.

Less dangerous, which they make up for by being that much more persistent, are the mosquitoes. Something visitors to both countries will become acquainted with. A tip: let the geckoes run around on the walls or ceiling of your room. The small lizard is not only absolutely harmless, but a first class mosquito trap.

Much more dangerous than the geckoes are the crocodiles, which one

Bengali Kingfisher

the walk is through the big Khielly Fish Market in Rangoon.

The same variety of species abounds in the air as in the water; the bird world is very obvious. Parrots and kingfishers are seen in the countryside outside the towns. Large birds however, such as the vulture, are only found in inaccessible places or in nature reserves such as Thailand's Khao Yai.

If, as is often said, the women of Thailand and Burma are as beautiful as butterflies, then they must be very beautiful indeed. These large, brilliantly marked insects will cause many a collectors heart to beat more rapidly.

With other flying insects on the other hand, especially in the vicinity of Sukhothai, people have other things entirely on their minds, and in particular as far as the flying beetles are concerned. They are attracted by light at night, trapped, cooked and mixed with a spicy paste. They are considered something of a delicacy and are never lacking at festive meals.

And the big animals? In addition to several types of apes and monkeys – take care when visiting the temple at Lopburi, they bite – tigers and leopards are said to exist in both countries. And in Burma they are said to be so numerous they can be hunted by country dwellers without permits. Bears, Banteng cattle, in Burma the Takin, larger than cattle and a member of the chamois family, rhinoceros, wild boar and tapir complete the range.

In addition to cats, water buffalo – and occasionally, elephants –, dogs, zebu (humped cattle) and poultry number among the domestic animals; horses are mainly kept in the Shan Mountains of Burma.

hardly sees any more in the wild; at a crododile farm around 25 km (15,5 miles) from Bangkok on the way to Pattaya, they can be seen in great numbers. And there is even said to be fights arranged between man and beast as a tourist attraction.

Fights of another kind take place in the water, namely the aquarium. The gambling passion of the Thais was what led to this strange, and picturesque practice; two fighting fish are placed in a small tank which in turn is placed on a large table in the village square. The fish fly at each other immediately and do everything they can to kill each other. After only a few minutes the fight ends with the death of one of the competitors, the punters richer or poorer by a few Baht.

The fishermen are at all events successful. In the Gulf of Siam, in Burma the Gulfs of Bengal and Martaban and in the inland waters as well, fish, fish and more fish. A morning stroll through the fish market supplies really photogenic instruction, in particular if

Wild Plants – The Flora

Figures vary; it is said that between 500 and 1,000 different types of orchids flourish in Burma and Thailand; cultivation of hybrids has been for

Siamese Lyre Deer
(Cervus eldi siamensis)

some time a hobby for many, and in particular the North of Burma would seem to be a treasure trove of orchids.

Nature lovers from more moderate climes will come into their own in the tropics. Even temperatures and sufficient rain ensure that wild vegetation flourishes even in the thin tropical humus soil, in almost confusing variety. One example; Rangoon's Bogyoke Aung San Park and the agricultural university Kasetsart close to Dom Muang Airport on the outskirts of Bangkok. There is no botanic garden as we understand it in the Thai capital.

Thailand can still be classified as being more than half covered by forests,

in spite of the destructive lumbering which has taken place. It has to be borne in mind however that the change between dry periods and rainy seasons as well as elevations bring forth considerable differences in the character of the forests.

On the South-east coast and the Malayan Peninsula there are evergreen rain forests; rainfall evenly distributed throughout the year of at least 2,000 mm (6'7") ensures enormous variety; climbing and parasite plants, ferns and lianas under a roof of leaves of the trees reaching up to 30 metres (98'5") in height. Even more impenetrable is the forest of mist which flourishes from heights of 1,800 metres (5,905 ft.) upwards.

In central and northern Thailand there are finally those areas, with extended dry periods, with the Monsoon forests, and trees which shed their leaves, typical of the country. It is here that timber companies find the sought after teak for export; the Yangs grow here too which supply the oils for lacquer. Another tree which is widespread is the bamboo. The Monsoon forest is less dense than the rain forests.

Oak and pine forests in the north of Thailand (up to 1,500 metres 4,921 ft.), coconut palms along sandy coasts and finally, the mangrove forests, which have sprouted in some 30 types on the swampy coasts, make up the forest riches of Thailand.

There's a lot of bustle around the teak docks of the ancient royal city of Burma, Mandalay. Everyday, from sunrise, several teams of water buffaloes pull and strain to extract the bulky teak

waddy Delta is 300 kilometres/186 miles wide). Evergreen rain forests with ironwood and andaman redwood in the mountainous regions and the humid coastal areas are countered by wide spread dry regions in the central plains, with hardly any trees. Cacti and thorn bushes are characteristic vegetation here.

Rhododendrons, more than 100 types, hibiscus, bougainvillea, acacia, lotus, frangipani, jacaranda, orchids and innumerable other flowers turn large sections of Burma and Thailand into natural botanic gardens and form blobs of bright colour in the monotonous green of the rice fields.

Epiphyte; plant which grows on another plant or tree and flourishes almost exclusively on "Light and Air".

trunks from the mud. Trucks transport these then on to the sawmills or to the ships which carry them abroad. Burma is, and will remain, one of the major exporters of teak around the world, and the work of man and beast is vital for the economy. The teak trees are felled in the Burmese monsoon jungles and then floated down to specific points from where they then start on the overland journey to the ports.

The British colonialists were well aware of the value of teak, which led as a result to indiscriminate felling, without reafforestation. But in spite of this Burma is covered by more than one half with forests.

Another major source of finance are the trees, up to 30 metres (98'5") in height, of the swamps which have spread in the main delta areas (the Irra-

Characteristic too are the various types of palms, which can also be used for practical purposes; the coconut palm for instance is the only tree capable of turning salt water into sweet water; and for this reason they are found in those places where sweet water is scarce or completely lacking. The Areca palm supplies the betel chewers (see separate chapter) with the indispensible nut and the sugar palm is a source of starch, sugar and wine.

Then there is only cotton to be named, plus – mainly in the south of Thailand – the rubber tree. Planted in huge plantations, the trunks of this tree from the family of the spurge, are scored and the sap processed as rubber. The cotton plants, up to 1 metre (3'3") in height, are not only recognisable from their large white and yellow blooms, they also give off a characteristic, pleasant, perfume.

The fibres of jute and Kenaf, found in the humid zones, plants which resemble cabbage reaching a height of up to 3 metres, are used for making sacks.

At all those places rich in vegetation, generous harvests of fruit are also guaranteed. For instance there are more than 30 different types of bananas; pineapples, melons, rambutans (resembling lichis); durians, guavas, mangoes, papayas, jambuse, mangosteens, star fruit and lichis enrich the menus of both countries in the most pleasant way.

Explosion without a Bang –
The Peoples of Thailand

It has happened in Thailand too, that soundless explosion. At present 45 million live here and in 20 years that figure will double; in 1950 the population numbered only 20 millions. The population exploded noiselessly, without a bang. Nevertheless it is not without danger. How are the increasing numbers to be fed?

Carniverous plant (Pitcher Plant)
(Nepenthes mirabilis)

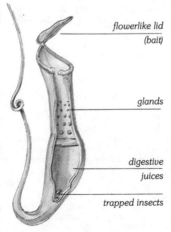

flowerlike lid
(bait)

glands

digestive
juices

trapped insects

Seventy percent still work today in agriculture; measured against the rising birthrate of 3% annually, the arable land is slowly dwindling. And this only represents an unproductive 30% of national income. Industry is still in its infancy – at least comparatively – and jobs don't keep pace with the increase of inhabitants. "Too many children keep you poor", this slogan sponsored by the government is justified in the "Land of the Free" (Muang Thai). A noiseless explosion.

The "Free" (Thai) have been known as a cultural people dating back centuries. The tribes known under this name are not only settled in Thailand, they include also the Shan of Burma (see separate chapter) and the 2.5 million Laotians of Laos, Vietnam and Kampuchea, plus the some 8 million inhabitants of the Chinese province Yunnan.

Anthropologically mainly of the palaeo-mongolian race, the Thais were pushed further and further South from this mountainous region of Yunnan, by the expanding "Middle Kingdom". Their probable original settlement area at the central Yangste had already been abandoned 2,000 B. C.

When in the middle of the 13th century the Thai realms of Nan-chao in

Yunnan were destroyed by the mighty Mongolian leader Kublai Khan, the small statured Thais finally gathered their goods and chattels, strapped on their walking shoes, and after several migrations reached, in the 13th century, that territory which is today Thailand.

Not all of them however set out on the long march South – the Thai people splintered; the northern Thais remained in Yunnan, the western group became the Shan settled in the east of Burma, the eastern Thais spread over several Chinese provinces and the north of Tonking; a fourth group were finally transformed into Siamese of the Menam plains, the Laotians of the Mekong valley and the Thai-Korat in the east.

These latter in all probability stem from armies of the 14th century who conquered wide stretches of Kampuchea.

Ideal conditions: the Menam plains, 100 by 500 km, became a favourite settlement area – flat, fruitful, easy to irrigate. For this reason the Thai of the Menam pushed their way as a wedge between the Khmer and Mon already settled here; they began to feel themselves financially and culturally superior to their relatives in the mountainous regions, and this in fact did apply, thus from the middle of the 14th century they created the focal point of the land, and today half of the population lives there.

A colourful mixture: when, from the 9th century on, the first forerunners of the Mongolian Thais, with their tonal language related to Chinese, reached Thai territory they did not settle in a vacuum, Mon and Khmer were settled here, further south, Malayans. The process of mixing took place – the modern Thai was born.

In the Thailand of today there are numerous ethnic minorities, mainly occupied as hill farmers, reckoned to number some 500,000. They spend their frugal lives for the most part in the villages of the North. Their national dress, customs, life and language distinguish them from the predominant Thais.

These mountain people who aim at being selfsupporting are divided into two groups from an aspect of language; the Sino-Tibetan, which covers the Akha, Lahu and Lisu plus – as an independent group – the Meo and Yao, and tribes of the Karen, and then the Austro-Asiatic group which includes the Khamu, Lawa and Htin who number among the Mon-Khmer races, these latter regard the Thai mountains as their rightful home, whereas the Sino-Tibetans only immigrated in the last 100 years, and still do.

Burning forests: The Akha, Yao, Meo, Lahu and Lisu cause the officials responsible for forestry in Bangkok considerable problems with the practice of clearing land for cultivation by fire. The soil is laid waste and exhausted after only a few years, with worthless bushes instead of trees which prevent erosion, the tribes then move on to the next mountainside; rice, maize, vegetables and opium ensure an income and food.

Compared with them, the Lawa, Khamu, Htin and Karen are more settled and cultivate terraces or wet rice fields.

Rebellious –
The Meo in Thailand

They are small in stature, but from another aspect really big; the Meo in Thailand, Vietnam, Laos and Burma have until the present time been able to hold on to political and cultural independence, at least to a certain degree. The some 500,000 people who call these lands home today represent only one third of the total Meo people; the greater part is still settled in the Chinese provinces of Szechwan, Kwangsi, Yunnan and Guizhou (Kwangchou). And their name is not the same all over either; in China they are called Miao, in Thailand actually Meau and only in Laos Meo. They only migrated to Indochina, from China in the last century after a revolt had been ruthlessly crushed by the Ching Dynasty.

But also here the people of the Sino-Tibetan family of languages were not left in peace. Rebellions were rapidly put down by the French colonialists and the Meo withdrew further into almost inaccessible regions. Today attempts are being made to integrate them peacefully into the respective state organisations but success varies; the Meo avoid all attempts or withdraw entirely.

The peaceful farmers are on the other hand active on the mountainsides which they clear by fire and plant with mountain rice, maize and opium for their own needs and sale. If one relies on official reports 1 kilo raw opium brings up to 100 dollars, and is still offered fairly openly even today, an amount which represents a fortune to the Meo and which is invested in silver bars and jewelry.

Status thinking, which is expressed above all by the men in riches in silver jewelry, simply cannot be eradicated in the small Meo villages, and horses too are another prestigious status symbol. Men live there in a culture strongly paternalistic, equally influenced by animistic and Chinese customs. Taoistic gods have entered into an alliance with those of nature, a Meo alliance, and by no means an unholy one…

Certain things are strictly taboo, including any form of in-breeding. Marriage may not take place within a clan, since however each village considers itself a clan marital partners have to be sought in other villages. Perhaps they observe this taboo so strictly because they regard themselves as the descendants of an incestuous relationship between siblings.

What appears at first to be comparative sexual freedom before marriage culminates in that much more restriction afterwards. Although the Meo male still has it good; if he can pay the bride price, he takes a second wife. Polygamy is widespread. The female is less fortunate. Should she be dissatisfied with her position in the wooden huts, which are built directly on the earth as opposed to many others on piles in other parts of Thailand, she only has the choice of moving to another village and thus leaving the clan.

Burial rites are carefully preserved and are intended to show the dead, whose bodies by the way are kept as long as possible, the way to the after-world to their ancestors. These are purely animistic in origin; drums and bamboo flutes accompany the mourners. Thus the deceased is prepared for reincarnation.

In the past the clothing of the Meo must have been colourful and imaginative, but today, the men at least, have caught up with modern times; the traditional black jacket is being replaced more and more by western clothing. The ladies on the other hand are more fashion conscious. Artistically draped turbans – hair at the forehead is simply shaved off – and richly embroidered black trouser suits indicate that the eternal female is also more strongly apparent in the Meo culture. Green and red sashes emphasize this.

Tourists will have the opportunity of visiting a Meo village in the region of northern Thailand Chiangmai. And perhaps one or two will also have the chance of buying an especially attractive example of handicrafts as proof of the skill of these people.

A village cuts itself off; the harvest festival is of major importance to the Lawa, they close their village to all outsiders and no one is permitted to leave. Young men have built two altars decorated with spears and swords. A bound pig stands before them. Each family brings a chicken, and several of these will be sacrificed. Then as a highpoint the pig is slaughtered, the meat distributed among the villagers.

The Lawa have built these villages in the mountains of North Thailand, close to the Burmese border. Here some 10,000 people live in accordance with ancient customs. A life which could undoubtedly be easier led on the plains. A legend, handed down through the ages tells them why they can't move there; their king had asked for the hand of the Mon queen in marriage; she however made a condition that first he had to throw a spear over a great distance as far as her palace. After the first unsuccessful attempt she gave him permission to try again, but a magic

headband which she was wearing had weakened him so much that he was almost unable to lift the spear. And he had to return to the mountains with his people.

In the eyes of the politicians in Bangkok these mountain peoples are ever an uncertain quantity. They, who have never had a very prominent leadership, have also no sense of nationality and thus are considered susceptible to political exploitation and worse, liable for political infiltration.

From 1959 the government has, for this reason, backed a type of welfare programme to support the mountain people in their development and to educate them into becoming good citizens; and an attempt is being made to draw them away from cultivation of opium. They still however are resisting any interference from Thai culture.

There is less trouble with the Chinese and Indians, seen by visitors all over in larger towns, but of course with major concentrations in Bangkok. Whilst the Indians are really successful as dealers in textiles and tailors, the approximately 4 million Chinese in Thailand dominate the small trades. Racial unrest, such as occurred in other countries of South-east Asia has been avoided so far, as the result of an exemplary aliens policy. Most Chinese in the meantime have Thai passports and many of them are married to Thai women. A healthy stock of multi-racial people is the result.

The situation is quite different with the Moslem Malayans in the southern provinces. Neither religion nor customs or language has been adopted from the Thais. Major aim of this people numbering some 1 million is a pilgrimage to Mecca and the Buddhistic culture of the Thais is completely alien. It is still unclear whether they will demand more autonomy from Bangkok, or even integration with Malaysia, sister state in the South.

With some 87 people per square kilometre (225 people per sq. mi.) Thailand is still considered today not over populated. And problems only arise with concentrations on the plains and the fruitful parts of the country. In these regions the limits of settlement have been reached, but 80% of all Thais still live in village communities and only the teeming Bangkok with bordering Thonburi can be described as cities.

What one notices most about the people of this country? More than their abiding politeness, perhaps their unaffectedness and friendliness towards farangs (strangers), a lesson in hospitality; and more; the casualness with which Thais regard many of those things in life which we think are indispensible. Things, which if one really gets down to rock bottom, that aren't so important after all. "Mai pen rai" says the Thai, it doesn't matter, it's not so important. With this "mai pen rai", many Thais have the last laugh over stressed Europeans.

Long Necks –
The People of Burma

Tourist marketing on a low budget: large, brightly coloured posters aimed at tempting visitors to Burma, the subject? Women of the Paduang with their necks grotesquely stretched by brass rings, the head, which then appears small in proportion, seems to crown a pillar of brass. But hardly any of the strangers are permitted to visit the villages in which the "Giraffe-necked Women" can be seen in the flesh. These are in the Kayah territory and out-of-

bounds for tourists. It won't however be very long before this exotic rite already dying out, is completely extinct.

Paduang, long necks, is the name of this Mongolian tribe, assimilated into the Karen, living on the borders to Thailand, who have fallen victim to this strange ideal of feminine beauty. The greater the number of rings and richer the material, the richer and respected the family of the wearer. In other words a sign of social status measured on the length of the neck: particularly eminent Paduang women can lay claim to a giraffe-like throat, three times longer than normal. It's perfectly clear that more and more young women today refuse to take part in this ancient cult. And only older women display their ringed necks with pride; in truth they really don't have much choice for the rings cannot be removed.

Unfaithfulness is punished by the Paduang men in their own special way, the rings are removed from the neck of the spouse. What would appear to be harmless at first glance is at second exposed as cruel punishment; the adulteress is condemned to spend the rest of her life in a supine position or have her head supported in some way, due to years wearing the brass rings, rarely gold, the neck muscles have atrophied and the cervical vertebrae are deformed.

In earlier times the Paduang girls were fitted with the first neck ring at the age of five. The day on which this important ceremony was to take place was laid down precisely in accordance with horoscopes drawn up by the Shamans of the village. And the day was a day of celebration for all with drinking and feasting. The girl's neck was smeared with a salve, whose ingredients are a closely guarded secret, and massaged for hours. Then the priest carefully fitted the spiral, while the mother held the child's head. Little cushions of material eased the pain and prevented rubbing. These are removed later.

At intervals of two years then the ring or spiral is replaced by a longer one, and the head became further and further removed from the shoulders. Similar rings, however without stretching, now also adorn arms and legs.

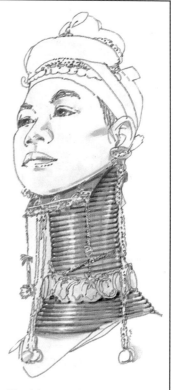

The elaborate neck rings as worn by the "long-necked women".

According to legend the rings were intended to protect against tiger bites in their original home, most probably in the North of China; these animals as is known spring at the throats of their victims. In fact however what is in reality involved is a rare type of initiation rite which can also be seen among some of the peoples of Africa.

Hitherto no one has been able to completely unravel the past of the Karen people, into whom the Paduang have also been assimilated. Skilled musicians with many rare and original instruments (frog drums) these tribes reached the south of Burma after several migrations and according to their own legends over the "River of Flowing Sand" (Huang Ho?). They almost certainly appeared on the soil of Burma before the present dominant Birmans and they represent, after these, the largest ethnic group numbering some 2 millions.

The Karen have not only been at loggerheads with the ruling Birmans since independence in 1948, with demands for greater autonomy or even their own state. Violent jungle clashes along the border to Thailand lend emphasis to these demands and the report of an Austrian journalist in a book, who accompanied the Karen rebels graphically illustrates the problem. And the situation is complicated further by the fact that the Karen are divided into two main groups White and Red Karen (which are once more sub-divided into smaller groups such as Sgo, Taundo), and are to a large extent Christians, which results in another point of friction with Buddhistic Burma.

In addition to the Karen, the Shan form the next largest minority in Burma. They live in a State of the same name, capital Taunggyi, and they demand the same rights as the Karen, namely independence.

The group, which is closely related racially to the neighbouring Thais, numbering around 1.5 millions is a member of the three main tribes – with the Thai of Thailand and the Lao in Laos – who with strong traces of Chinese blood, speak the Sino-Thai dialect.

These three peoples were first mentioned 1,300 years ago when their common ruler Kolofeng of Nan Chao allied himself with Tibet against the Chinese.

The reconstructed migration of these peoples is long. Originally they trickled into the plains of the Yangtse from their central Asiatic settlements. From there the journey went further south to Nan Chao in the "southern provinces." Thus the realms lay in what is today the southern Chinese province of Yunnan. In 1253 however the Mongolian hordes of Kublai Khan rang the death knell for Nan Chao; the Thai peoples moved on again further South.

The Birman Pagan kingdom had passed its zenith, Cambodias Angkor (Khmer) were disintegrating, Cham was only an historical legend – there was no one to stop them. And in this way they came to establish the first realms, which were only of local significance (see separate chapter).

At the same time further to the West, on Burmese soil, the first kingdoms were established by the Shan, who call themselves "Tai". After the downfall of the Birman kingdom of Pagan, provoked by arrogance, the way was free for the Shan to take over regency of large parts of the country. Divided into princedoms, they dictated the affairs of this region until the middle of the 16th century; Bayinnaung put an end to this state of affairs and made the Birmans the dominant people once more. The Buddhistic Shan, whose religion is interspersed with a strong belief in ghosts, were never again to regain power.

But they were unwilling to live under the yoke of the Birmans, their weakness was always a tendency to splinter into small princedoms (mong) which not seldom were also feuding with each other. Each sabwah (prince) attempted to gain absolute power with his followers and the Shan were never able to create a unified system of politics and military authority. After grant of independence the government in Rangoon without any ado, combined 44 Shan states to form one special territory for their nationality.

The Shan once more were the source of political unrest. Already in 1960 turbulent events took place at the conference called by the Shan prince, Sao Taike at Taunggyi; shrill anti-Burmese voices were heard and representatives of other ethnic minorities – Karen, Chin and Kachin – left the conference in irritation.

And then not only the call for autonomy was loud in the Shan mountains, independence was the new motto and a signal for Rangoon to act fast. General Nu Win from then on the strong man in the land, took over the reins of office from the Prime Minister U Nu – who tended towards conciliation with the Shan – in a bloodless coup in 1962 and turned the military screws tighter as far as the rebellious Shan were concerned. Even today there is still only an uneasy calm.

What remained; the Shan wrap their complete helplessness against the power of the Birmans in a legend, a legend which reveals the full extent of their disappointment; long, long ago a Shan prince wished to settle with his subjects at the well filled rice bowl of the central Irrawaddy plains. Since however the Birmans had already spread there he sent emissaries to their king with the request that he and his people be allowed to settle. The Birman regent must have been a very good diplomat – his proposal, Birmans and Shans were to enter into a religious competition; both peoples were to build a pagoda. Should the Shan complete theirs first then the way was open to the Irrawaddy plains, otherwise things would remain as they were.

Eagerly and skillfully the Shans spent all night building their stone pagoda, when day broke they saw in the pale light the silhouette of the completed pagoda of their opponents. Disappointed they withdrew from the scene of their defeat. What they didn't know was that the wily Birmans had built their pagoda of wood – and simply painted it white.

The Shan were more successful in other places, and it is said that the original name of Thailand, Siam, comes from the kingdom of Syam; or is derived from a Shan word.

The stranger will hardly ever have the opportunity to make contact with other ethnic minorities in Burma. They live either in territories which are extremely inaccessible, or areas which are out-of-bounds for tourists.

A meeting with them would at all events be interesting since they differ considerably in their culture from the Birmans, Karen or Shan. It is said of the Wa for instance, that even today they swarm out from their fortified villages in the north-easterly Shan mountains on ritual head hunts. And the Nagas in the jungles at the foot of the Himalaya chain display strangely attractive tattoos; these are reputed to be illustrations of human heads which changed "owners" during disputes with neighbouring villages; they are however extremely friendly towards strangers. The antics of the young Naga girls before marriage would in all probability bring red to the cheeks of even our much less than backward city teenagers.

The Arakans live between the two worlds of Asia, those of the Indians and Tibeto-Birmans, a condition which gave them independence until 1784 – in spite of several wars. Their territory only opens towards India whilst in the direction of Burma there is a natural barrier in the shape of the Arakan Mountains. The Arakans who represent about 1% of the population were possibly already settled in the country before the Birmans and in all probability assumed Buddhism before these too.

There has been hardly any friction between the Birmans and the Tibeto-Burmese Chin (2% of total population) or the Kachin (2.2%), but this is explained by the very loose connections which exist between these. The men of these peoples gained great respect as soldiers in the Anglo-Indian army and the animistic believers in ghosts are also represented in the Burmese armed forces.

Indians and Chinese (1% of the pop.) plus Mon, the remains of a people speaking Khmer round off the picture of the ethnic divisions of Burma. A picturesque picture which has however, for centuries, been dominated by the strong colours of the Birman people.

The phase of flourishing culture on Burmese soil was rung in by the Pyu, in the meantime extinct, and the Mon; but soon these "greatest arch-enemies of the Birmans", as they are described in literature, will also die out; they met the vitality and pragmatism of the Birmans with composure and tolerance, and were thus able to infiltrate the culture of the Birman subduers, but were unable to maintain their position as dominant people. Their influence on Birman culture is apparent at every turn, most noticeably in the architecture. Burma without the Mon would be pragmatism without intellect.

The Birmans, and there is no doubt about this, are the masters in a state which is torn by many particular interests, they however, who marched their feet sore through the Gobi Desert in the West and on the rocky paths of Tibet, and who have made toughness and vitality major features of their national character, have been able to prevent those special interests tearing the land apart.

At the present time the Birmans, who make up two thirds of the total population of 34 millions, are mainly settled in the rice basket of the country; in the central plains of the Irrawaddy and the delta regions of the South. They are also members of the Tibeto-Birman family as are the Chin and Kachin, also from an aspect of language: their original home was most likely somewhere between the Gobi and the North-east section of Tibet.

From the 8th/9th century they trickled into the South and settled at the central area of the dry, but fruitful, mighty Elephant River (Irrawaddy) at which there has been no elephants for quite some time now. It was easy to irrigate the dry soil with river water and cultivate the land, a condition which assisted the Birmans greatly, accustomed as they were to cultivate wet rice. Two or three centuries later the Birman settlement spread throughout the valley of the Sittang as far as the coast and towards the West over the Arakan Mountains to the Gulf of Bengal.

115

Singing Speech –
Painted Writing

Even among those foreigners who have spent many years in Thailand, or Burma, many have hoisted the white flag of despairing surrender; they will never master the language perfectly and the same applies to the written language.

Even although compared with the spoken language, the written is relatively simple. And fairly young. The Birmans grasped the advantage in the 11th century, conditions were settled militarily and politically, their Pagan realms spread throughout Burma as the first Birman empire; but culturally they were still lagging and for this reason the beaten Mon were elevated to the rank of teachers. And on this occasion the Mon script was also adopted, which was related to the southern Indian Pali, and even today still bears resemblance to the Telugu script of southern India.

It was clear though; the Birman feeling for the artistic changed also the script over the centuries, it is rounder, painted from left to right, without spaces in 12 vowels and 33 consonants, without symbols.

Thai writing is even younger and here too the Mon set the pattern, and to some extent also the Khmer, who for their part had made use of southern Indian sources. King Ram Khamheng (1280–1317) the courageous founder of Sukhothai, created from this the new Thai alphabet; running to the right without differentiation between capitals and small letters and without spaces,

Colonial subjection of Burma by the British started around the middle of the 19th century and had the effect of regulating distribution of the population; the unhealthy, swampy delta of the Irrawaddy in the South, in Lower Burma, had until then remained almost unsettled. Since however the new colonial masters were interested in cultivating rice close to the coast they encouraged settlement in the giant delta region: plots of land up to around 6 hectares were given to farmers free of charge.

Prospects of land in this part of the country blessed with heavy rainfall led many Birman families into migrating

South. The Delta became the most densely populated region and today, together with the neighbouring Sittang Delta, houses one quarter of the population.

And not only Birmans let themselves be tempted by the prospects of a better life. Shan, Chin and, above all, Karen too, moved into the area so that the Delta became the largest part of Burma with a multi-racial population; Indians and Chinese complete the colourful palette.

The political importance kept step with policy on population, Rangoon be-

which traditionally only indicated the end of a sentence, recently however symbols have been used in sentences, 44 consonants (including five different forms of "s") and 32 vowels which are placed before, behind, above or below the consonants, form a rounded picture.

It's the tone that makes music; in the Thai language it is five tones which dominate speech and make up the sound pattern, and which make communication possible at all. In reading it is five intonations. When the Thai came from southern China they of course brought their own language with them, they were members of the Sino–Tibetan family of languages and were combined with the Chinese in the group of the Sino-Thai language. Mainly one syllable, high pitched language with five nuances, somewhat more pleasant to the ear than Chinese. In Thailand they met up with Mon and Khmer and adopted words from these peoples too; later still certain elements of Sanskrit and Pali were added. Taking all these influences together: Thai is a Chinese language translated into Indian letters; one does have to listen very carefully.

Burmese is as Chinese also a single syllable, tonal, language and there are certainly close resemblances with Thai; the language of the Birmans, today official language of the country, counts among the Tibeto-Birman sub-group of the Sino-Tibetan family of languages, although in this case there are only three different pitches. According to the last count in 1931 (!) 131 different languages were spoken in addition to Birman, this is particularly obvious among the Shan, Chin, Kachin and Karen. But all in all some 80% of the population has caught up with the times and speaks (in addition) Birman, which most probably one should now call Burmese, as the national language. In Burma the same applies as in Thailand – spoken and written languages stem from different cultures.

came capital in 1885, up to this time, dictated by London, the Birmans had clung to their old centres of political and religious power.

There only remains a word or two to be said on the original inhabitants of a land which was settled relatively late by those peoples and tribes mentioned. Only very little is known. Around 25 years ago pygmies of Chinese origin were discovered in the Himalayas of Burma, who called themselves Tarong. Their religion included a belief in Heaven and Hell, but whether negritoes – as is the case in other parts of Southeast Asia – were also the first humans to inhabit Burma will never really be clarified, their traces, with the exception of a few archaeological finds of stone fragments, have long been erased...

ABC of Good Manners

Please, please, always keep in mind that the Thais, and Burmese, number among those peoples who will forgive many a faux pas on the part of a visitor unfamiliar with habits and customs, but for whom aggresiveness, even when it appears justified in our eyes, is a sign of an absolute lack of tact and good manners; the louder you are and the more you argue, the less you'll achieve; and what's more you lose face.

There are a few rules of etiquette, easy to remember, which make contact between the guest and hosts (these are the natives) less difficult and even rewarding.

In Thailand criticism, or jokes, of, or involving the Royal Family, are strictly taboo; the Thai King is not only the religious leader – in the same way as the Queen of England, Defender of the Faith – but for many Thais still subconsciously the God King. Even that which the Thais themselves criticize may not be voiced in public. The King is shown on banknotes and should you have the misfortune to drop one, take care not to tread on it, you could touch the picture of the King with your foot.

If you are travelling as a single man you can, and welcome, find yourself a Thai girl-friend during your stay in Thailand, and don't be put off by the tirades launched by some women's movements who see in this exploitation of Thai women; this is nonense "based" on a complete lack of knowlegde of the real facts. But avoid all forms of physical contact in public; ranging from holding hands to a pat on the shoulder; this is a defamation of your friend and yourself. You will be seen as an ill-man-

nered lout. Don't ever touch a Thai – not even a child – on the head, this is considered the seat of the soul, and holy, and for this reason you should never reach anything over anyone's head.

Women have to be specially careful towards monks. They may not be touched, and on some occasions they may not even be spoken to.

European type of greetings are accepted in Thailand. If you want to be really polite, then try it in the language of the land – but properly; otherwise you might just look silly. "Sawaddi" is said at all times of the day and at the same time the head bowed slightly with the hands, palms together, before your nose. Only high ranking persons are greeted with the hands level with the forehead; and hands together at mouth level is reserved for those of an inferior status.

Most Europeans and other visitors are judged first by their clothes. Shorts are only worn by Thai males on the beach or by those who can't afford any others. A man in shorts and white legs doesn't only amuse the natives! All too revealing clothing for the ladies is by the way frowned on – which seems strange in a country where the girls are seen on the beaches in scanty tangas (but just ask about those girls!). And one other thing about dress: shoes may not be worn in the temples; some people resort to so-called "temple-socks" which not only tend to look unintentionally funny, but are also a slight to the Thais; even if you are a little afraid of "catching something" – which could happen anyplace anyway – leave your socks at home.

Polite, One and All

Absolutely polite, still a reality in Burma and Thailand. This politeness is also expressed verbally in both countries. Above all when addressing each other, and is more than a mere "madam" for instance.

U Thant was secretary general of UNO, U Nu a leading politician. The U binds them, but has nothing to do with relationship. For, depending on age, regard and position, the Burmese man is addressed with U, Ko or Maung. U is subject to power and faith; anyone so called is a man with influence. Ko means brother and is used under those of equal standing, Maung is for someone younger or a small boy.

Then there is in Burma, Bo and Thakin too. Officers make use of the first, while Thakin which means "master" is somewhat equal to the English "Sir".

Care has to be taken with the word Mi towards women. This expresses affection; and when you address an older woman with Ma she would at most smile at the compliment for this is reserved for young women, the title Daw is used for the older generation.

The Thai language has a whole range of words to express politeness towards each other without having any specific meaning. The most important are Krap, used by men, and Ka, used by the ladies; if you want to be really polite then every question, every answer, every thank you has to be concluded with Krap or Ka. Absolute politeness, politely expressed.

As far as feet are concerned the Thai and Burmese are very sensitive. A scientist at the end of the last century really put his foot (both of them) in it in Mandalay; he was a guest of the King at the royal palace, was given a princely room and arranged his bed so that it pointed at the foot end towards the royal bedchamber. He was lucky to escape the next morning with a whole skin and there were no more signs of friendship from the King; which means in plain words: you never touch anyone with your foot, you don't point at anyone with your foot, you don't stamp your foot and you don't cross your legs in such a way that your foot points at the person opposite you.

On the whole rules on good manners are probably more strict in Burma than in Thailand. Which of course does not apply to the Royal Family, since there hasn't been one in Burma anyway for more than 100 years, or to contact between the sexes, since even the most stubborn playboy would have difficulty in getting to know the female of the species in Burma more than superficially. However rules for contact with monks, for visits to temples for general behaviour (see under Anahdeh) must be strictly observed.

If you are interested in the people of this country, if you should try to make closer contact, then the approach has

No, maybe – or: Maybe, no

Anahdeh: more than just a word, a feeling, and untranslatable. If Anahdeh is not understood, then the Burmese are not understood. Anahdeh is a sort of filter of all human relationships in Burma. And in this way a "no" becomes a maybe or even a maybe, no. All of Burmese politeness is hidden behind this one small word. Our definite "no" is avoided and other people are placed in a position of not having to use it either. When something is maybe possible, then that means it is impossible. Two people approach each other and meet halfway, no one loses face – Anahdeh makes it possible. Anyone new to the culture of Asia will have difficulty. The Burmese on the other hand use it to avoid difficulty. The reverse side of the coin is that Anahdeh not only helps to overcome the small irritating things of everyday life in that people don't confront each other with the unadorned truth; it also serves in making nothing of delays or weaknesses, as an excuse. The lazy uses Anahdeh as a shield – he didn't want to step on anyone's toes, and for that reason he couldn't do this, that or the other. Anahdeh – don't blame him for it.

to be made very carefully, very considerately, even when something, or nothing, works out the way you expected it to. If you then can put aside our western tendency to rush things, and adopt some of the Asiatic "there's time for everything", then you will surely meet up with a people who count among the most hospitable, most charming and cleanest in the world; average amount of soap used in Thailand per head lies eight times higher than in Europe (and not only because of the climate). Sawaddi…

Marionettes hang on 60 Strings – and dance

An almost unique, and independent art form, is being sold out in Burma; the puppet theatre. The artistically carved and splendidly clothed puppets are finding their way more and more frequently into the baggage of foreign tourists. Films have ousted "yoke thay pwe", the artistic play with strings, at whose ends dangle the marionettes, perhaps not lifelike, but at least bearing some semblance; today people would rather go to the cinema than to the puppet theatre, the meaning is lost…

This independent Burmese art form is based on an fairly young tradition of only 200 years, but nevertheless it flourished. "You dance just like a puppet", there was no greater compliment for a dancer. Why, is at least indicated in the short show near the Pagan Museum; with a masterly touch on up to 20 strings – even the puppets' eyebrows move in the time to the music – life is injected into the figures. Only a little imagination and the illusion is perfect. Dancers couldn't be better. Many figures in Burmese dance originated in the movements of the puppets, and not vice versa.

Burma is probably the only land on earth which had a Ministry of Theatre under the cruel, but artistically minded, King Bodawpaya (1781–1819). He however hung on a silken thread; he loved puppet play and encouraged it. And so it came about that real masters of the art could manipulate up to 60 strings, today anyone who can handle 20 is considered good.

Scientists have tried to trace the roots of Burmese puppet theatre in India, China or even Japan but according to the latest knowledge, it is believed that the art was developed in Burma itself, to perfection. A classic show lasts from sundown one evening to sun-up the next morning and is introduced by offering tributes in fruits and flowers to the theatre spirit, in order to keep him in an benevolent mood throughout. He is after all responsible for the success of the show.

Puppet shows started really cautiously. With pious Buddhistic texts the faithful public was to be shown the true way to knowledge. The inventive Burmese however soon found out that puppets could do something which wasn't allowed in prudish Burma, namely male and female appearing at the same time on the stage. The erotic un-

dertones created in this way acted as a stimulant for rapid development; the artistically manipulated puppets finally mirrored real life. When a new puppet was introduced into a piece then the puppeteer checked carefully that the expression fitted into his ensemble.

The performance lasting hours is accompanied by a real orchestra and the puppets' movements follow the singers. Each figure has its own specially dedicated music so that the audience knows before its appearance on the stage, who appears next. Only a few decades ago at least 20 figures formed the basis of every ensemble. But soon the puppets will be no more.

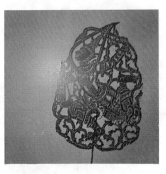

Shadow Play

A sport becomes dance. During Burmese Chinlon the natives demonstrate that they are great ball players without the tradition of football. The woven ball is kept in the air with feet and shoulders, it must not be allowed to touch the ground; the best players are found in real championships. In the championship class too are those who appear in the evening shows at the Karaweik Restaurant in Rangoon.

Traditional dances of the Pyu, Mon, Shan and Birmans have merged to become what is now Burmese dance. This would however be much poorer by many movements and expressions without Thai influence. For the Thais were the great teachers of dance as far as the Birmans are concerned, and unintentionally. In the 16th, and once again in the middle of the 18th century the magnificently decorated war elephants of the Birmans were on the march towards Ayutthaya. Sweet bounty of bitter wars: Siamese dancers, who not only mastered up to 500 hand movements and 84 different eye movements, but could also recite the great Indian epos of heroes and love of Rame and Sita, Hanuman and Rahwana (Ramayana) in dance.

They gave background to the Birman expressive dances and some believe, grace too.

Living classicism is what experts call the court dances of the Thai (khon).

Thai dancing.

Each movement is in accordance with strict rules. Masks, heavy paint and costumes which are as gorgeous as they are tight – in the past the dancers had to be sewn in – are all intended to wipe out individuality, or at least push it into the background. With the golden headdresses, these dances, which were never purely for pleasure – and never really popular among the people – fit into the general picture of court life and for years trained dancers performed there with that grace which has become with time synonymous with Thai women.

Quite possibly khon would have become extinct if the Royal Family had not founded an institute in Bangkok which teaches this traditional dance. This "Department of Fine Arts" also trains those dancers who appear in various restaurants, in what are strongly watered down performances.

More popular among the ordinary people were, and are, lakhon and likay. The personal interpretation of events in dance is given much wider scope and clowning is a firm element, above all in likay; coarse pieces in between make sure that the public gets what it wants even late into the night, and it's all really quite harmless anyway. While lakhon is danced without masks likay is seen as being the popular version of classic dance.

Buddhism –
of the Old School

It all started around 2,500 years ago with the son of a Nepalese prince. His sense of justice appeared to make it impossible for him to accept the strict caste system of the ruling Brahmans as something which was the will of God. He became the founder of a new religion. Buddhism made powerful advances and flourished in India and the neighbouring countries as the way of truth, as a form of human self-purification. Guatama, Siddhartha, Tatagatha, were some of the names of the founder. We call him "Buddha".

But anyone can, and should, be Buddha; many have been, and many will come. Buddha – is the Enlightened, and enlightenment in the form of the recognition of the "four pure truths" of suffering is to be attained by everyone.

Buddha was born some 560 B.C. in what is today southern Nepalese Terai. Reared with all the pomp and splendour of his aristocratic position in those times, it became clear to him –

so the legend – at the age of 29 on four occasions whilst riding out with his favourite horse, how senseless his life had been, Buddha encountered suffering; he met a beggar, a sick man, he saw a putrefying body and met an ascetic. He grasped the basic principles of Buddhism – all is suffering, because nothing lasts. Breaking with this vicious circle, dominated by rebirth, achieving Nirvana with death, were propagated as highest aims.

Buddha died at the age of 80. He left the world a legacy, which he formulated during his life and which is considered still today to be summed up in what was his first sermon to his favourite disciples. Only after years of asceticism and meditation did he express his "four pure truths":

– the recognition of suffering,

– suffering is caused by the thirst for life, desire,

– eliminating the cause of the thirst,

A Courageous Monk

Shin Arahan is 20 and seeks in the forests around Pagan, as an hermit, the true Buddhistic path to enlightenment. The peaceful life of the son of a Brahman priest of the Mon capital Thaton, is rudely disrupted. He meets a hunter who, in spite of the poor clothes of the young man, sees his religious power.

And in this way Shin Arahan reaches the court of the king of Pagan, the mighty ruler, Anawrahta. The King decides however to put him to the test and leads the ragged hermit into the throne room and tells him to take a seat, any place he likes. Shin Arahan seats himself on the throne and – under the law – sets his life at risk. Anawrahta however is not only a mighty ruler, but also a wise one, and acknowledges that Shin Arahan had not taken his place on the throne for himself but for his religion. The year is 1044, Hinayana Buddhism has set its foot in Burma.

So much for the legend. And it is not all that far removed from the historical truth. When Anawrahta took the throne of Pagan in 1044 there was among the Birmans a mixed religion of animism, Hinduism and Mahayana-Buddhism; tantric cults with the practice of magic, especially among the Ari monks, appeared to the ruler to be unsuitable for the young kingdom.

He converted under the teachings of Shin Arahan to Therawada Buddhism (= Hinayana) but still did not have enough power to put an end to the practices of the monks and introduce the new religion. The King of Thaton, Manuha, did have these powers in the form of the "Tripitaka" written records of Buddhism. Anawrahta's request for a copy was rejected and war elephants were set in march towards Thaton. The Mon kingdom was conquered and the "Tripitaka" carried back to Pagan in triumph on 30 elephants. In this way Hinaya Buddhism was established in Burma, a peaceful religion brought into full power by way of a war.

– The Way ("Noble 8-fold Path") which leads to this.

Buddha's religion was a reform movement which was aimed at changing the ancient Brahman culture of India. Religious orders for monks were founded which were followed, during Buddha's lifetime, by orders for nuns.

However prior to his death – in accordance with teachings – he was unable to appoint a successor and nothing was handed down in writing. Thus shortly after his death there were various schools of thought which differed from each other in dogmatics and disciplines.

The oldest of these schools is Therawadas, which still flourishes in Ceylon, Thailand and Burma. It is also called Hinayana (= small vehicle) whereby self-redemption (later regarded as too egoistic) is the major aim.

At the beginning of our age there then came into being the powerful Mahayana (= great vehicle) which became the actual world religion of Buddhism. Some 500 years later the Vajrayana was created after the meeting of Mahayana with the religions of the Himalayas from which there developed the sects with red and yellow head coverings of Lamaism.

Three councils which took place before time as we calculate it laid down the principles of Hinayana. These were followed by three others, two much later in Burma, and the last only some three decades ago in Rangoon.

The main theme of Buddhistic belief is that of Karma, which the faithful see as being an evaluation of all life's events – each act, thought and feeling – in some form or other. Everyone creates his own Karma. And when one dies then the Karma is reborn in a new existence as in a new outer; in this way everyone has it in his own hands to determine his next life, for better or worse...

... or already in his earthly life to find the Buddhistic knowledge of the truth of suffering and thus out of the circle of rebirth and death once more. The extinction of Nirvana is the aim which transcends all suffering.

The Buddhism of Thailand and Burma knows two "regions" in its cosmology, one is described as the "Region of Desire" in which animals, humans, spirits, demons, and gods too, live; they are all subject to transmigration, and the laws of Karma dictate the form of rebirth. The symbol of the various forms of existence in this region is the wheel, which is symbolically displayed on many religious buildings. There is over this only the goal of Nirvana.

But how is this to be reached? Man must see that all is suffering because transitory; the first of the "Four Truths" speaks of this: desires are the cause of all suffering (second truth); they are overcome by discipline (third truth) the right path to suppression of the cause of suffering is shown by the fourth truth. And in the end there is the redeeming knowledge obtained through meditation; consciousness of all former existences, to discern the Karma laws, to discern the four truths.

And the circle closes, for, the fourth of the four truths opens the way to extinction of suffering – transmigration is broken, Nirvana is reached.

Hands and Legs –
Speaking Buddha

Whilst in India the mighty Gupta dominated, in the 4th/5th centuries A.D. those effigies of Buddha emerged in the temples of Thailand and Burma which today, only slightly changed, lend that dignity, that withdrawnness, which often results in intangibility and lack of understanding on the part of people of other beliefs. But Buddha communicates with Buddhists; with his hands, his limbs, with all his physical characteristics.

Strict iconographical rules, forced, and still force, the Buddhistic artist to follow specific presentations in sculpture or painting. Whilst among Christians the sculptor is expected to show his creative self in for instance a crucifix, the Burmese or Thai sculpts a Buddha so that the observer – in addition to a specific message – also grasps clearly the nature of a religion of suffering; the artist therefore remains in the background, without giving up his talents for design or interpretation entirely, it is just that the scope is limited.

Thirty-two great characteristics, all signs of supernatural origin and supernatural powers, elevate the Buddha above the level of the rest of humanity.

Starting at the head: at the top of the skull a protuberance as the seat of special spiritual abilities, called Ushnisha by the experts, which probably is based on the hair dressing of the ascetics. Uma, originally a lock of hair twisted clockwise, has shrunk to become only a lighter spot or a rounded rise, symbolizes the mythical eye. The ears with the elongated lobes point towards Buddha's youth when the children of the rich wore heavy earrings; evil powers were to be prevented from entering the body here. In Buddhism however the long ears serve in hearing the inner voice. Three neck folds, a somewhat bizarre ideal of beauty, are considered a sign of luck. Closely curled hair and slim fingers bending back in conjunction with a simple robe which is only indicated and for the most part leaves the left shoulder bare, complete the requirements, which in Burma are only really complete when the face has the shape of a mango stone and the arms those of an elephant's trunk.

The Buddha has to be shown thus. But he still doesn't speak, gives no message. This is imparted through the position of the hands (mudra) and seated posture of the body (asana). In Thailand and Burma there are six basic mudras which can be supplemented by others more rare or varied too. Bhumipasha is the most important which is shown in the great majority of portrayals. Just before his enlightenment the historic Buddha touched the Earth with his right hand to call her, in his dispute with Mara – the buddhistic devil – as a witness of his will to spread his teachings among the people.

The gesture of meditation (dhyanimudra), that of preaching (dharmacakramudra) and argumentation (vitarka-mudra) are on show as exhibits at the National Museum in Bangkok. Then there are also the mudras of protection (abhaya) and giving/granting favours (varada).

In addition to the position of the hands, the seated posture is also important. And here too there are – with variations – basic positions. Legs crossed with soles of both feet upwards, shows the Buddha in the important lotus position (padma-asana); the Sassanid position shows both legs on the ground (bhadra-asana), and the two poses which demonstrate royal ease or spontaneity are the "playful posture" (lalitha-asana) where the right leg touches the inside of the left thigh, and "royal grace" (maharaja-lila) where the soles of both feet, raised above the ground, touch.

There are in both Thailand and Burma the "reclining" Buddhas. Mostly monumental figures which demonstrate to the faithful the gliding of the Enlightened One into Nirvana.

Sculptures of lacquered wood, or gilded, of brass, gold or papiermache, which is reinforced with cloth, in all cases effigies with a message.

Names, Names, and still more Names – Temples, Architecture

What is recognised in Burma immediately is only seen at second glance in Thailand. The strong religious devotion of the people. Nevertheless the Thais live no less intensely according to Hinayana-Buddhism (see separate chapter).

Expressive of the faith of the Thai and Burmese are the many temples and monasteries which are spread throughout both lands. These are said to number 24,000 in Thailand alone, and in Burmese Mandalay there is one pagoda for each 12 inhabitants. Hardly a village therefore in which there is no Wat or pagoda. Not all of them are documents of skilled artistic ability, but monuments of a deep faith at all events.

Chedi

Variety doesn't have to be confusing, although a little knowledge is a great help in understanding Thai and Burmese sacral buildings. Wat, Chedi, Mondhop, Viham, Prang, and so on are not merely different expressions for a certain style of building, on the contrary they signify character and function.

Burmese styles developed in the 12th century during the powerful Pagan Dynasty. And today the Pagoda, as final stage of the development, is what marks the character of the various towns and villages. It was the art of Burmese architects which made of Indian and Ceylonese originals – heavy, solid, arched over the earth – ethereal pagodas soaring heavenwards, and in spite of their mass, gothically appealing. In Thailand development was driven to hitherto unknown peaks, in every sense of the word. Thin needlelike spires which pierce the blue tropical skies. The Thais call their pagodas Chedi, the Burmese, Dagon; they are called Stupa by scientists. Four terms for just one building.

Indian, Ceylon and the ancient cultural peoples of Mon and Pyu were the godfathers as it were in the creation of the Thai and Burmese pagodas; this has been proven by archaeologists. What is less clear is where the word Pagoda originated. Chinese and even Portuguese sources have at times been gone into as possibilities, but the most likely explanation is that pagoda comes from the Ceylonese "dagoba" – with the consonants changed round. Dagoba is used to describe a chamber where relics are kept and just this is the traditional function of the Pagoda.

A mighty shrine for relics, striving heavenwards and ending in a steeple or peak. A lotus blossom turned upside down symbol of enlightenment on the head of Buddha – no matter how the appearance of the pagoda is interpreted – only one thing is really important; the structure itself, and even the relics carefully stored here in a chamber (hair, teeth, splinters of bone, scraps of material alleged from Buddha or his disciples, holy scriptures etc.), are hardly subjects of worship, not comparable with a Christian church. When Buddhists nevertheless pray at pagodas – which is seen frequently – then they are not acting in accordance with Buddhistic dogma; Buddha has entered Nirvana, prayers for blessings are therefore in vain. Tributes for the cleansing of their own souls are what the faithful can offer at the pagodas.

This is best done before a statue of Buddha; the significance of the pagoda itself is obvious; an expression of elevation – and with that a symbol for the doctrine. The path of the doctrines can be followed, the pagoda on the other hand remains untrodden.

Externally there are major differences between Thai and Burmese pagodas. And if one takes western tastes into account then most probably the Burmese are the more attractive. Five sections characterize the structure: the square base, with above the bell-like stupa (very often decorated with bo leaf designs) then the peak of the stupa, the shroud studded with precious stones (hti, symbol of the Holy One) and finally the jewelled point (seinbu); decorative markers and concentric rings at the end of the stupa (rice bowl symbol) are also used.

The Thai Chedi is less strongly defined architecturally but more than merely similar in design and function also a bell-like shrine, whereby the er ends in a square shaped walk (for instance for attaching holy flags); the tower-like structure rises above this ending in a peak, structured with concentric circles. While the large brick pagodas of Burma are frequently gold plated, the Thai were already at an early date, following Chinese tradition, covered with glazed tiles.

The type of building which most closely compares with Christian churches is the Burmese temple. This is always in the immediate vicinity of the pagoda and its importance emphasized by the figures of Buddha (see separate chapter). For the most part the roofs of these temples are terraced and crowned with a peak. Frequently however – in an architectural sense – the temples are more than just an annex to the pagoda. The best example of this where the temple becomes the predominant sacral feature is found at the Mon-Burmese Ananda Temple of Pagan.

Temples and pagodas – with stairways, meditation halls, resting places for pilgrims, accommodation for monks and bazaars for devotional objects, these are the main features of Birman architecture. Thailand has gone a step further with its Wats. Almost all holy places in the country are connected to Wats, the monasteries. The monks live and teach here and care for the buildings; lecture rooms and libraries, ordination rooms and cloisters are a must.

Then there is a whole range of structures which characterize the monastery area of the Wat.

On the other hand all these buildings don't have to be provided at all Wats.

Mr. Stately and
Miss Golden Face

The life of the faithful Burmese is determined by Buddhism – and animist spirits; the 37 most important of these ghosts, Nats, as they are called, have their home at Mount Popa around 50 km (31 miles) south-east of Pagan.

Ancient religious myths, legends and philosophy are woven into a Southeast Asian fairytale more than 1,000 years old, which came to an end at 1,518 metre (4,924 ft.) high andesite peak of the Popa volcano.

But before the tale starts some information which is for the Burmese only the reverse side of the same coin, but for us seems all that more important because it makes the fairytale just that much more fabulous. As late as 1961 the former prime minister U Nu made a pilgrimage to the Nats at Popa to ask for their help in fending off a national crisis; U Nu toppled from power one year later; but the tale was reality for U Nu as were the Nats.

According to legend 442 B.C. there was a severe earthquake in Central Burma, Popa broke through the barren earth and became petrified as a gigantic lava rock after reaching 1,000 metres (3,280 ft.). Volcanic ash made the slopes fruitful and soon flourished in the most beautiful colours in the midst of the monotonous brown of the plain. Popa, flower, the colossus was named in Sanskrit.

And now to the fairytale: the blacksmith U Tin De was the strongest man in the land, he lived at the village of Tagaung and was loved by all; when his hammer struck the anvil the whole earth shook. He was called Mr. Stately by the others.

The main cultic function is also performed by the Chedi at the Wats, then there are two buildings which are in direct relationship to the community of monks; Bot and Viharn (Sanskrit: monastery). The most esteemed is the smaller of the two, the Bot; this is reserved for ordination ceremonies of the monks and symbolically cordoned off from the rest of the surroundings by eight Bai Semas, holy stones in the form of the bo leaves. These really should number nine (Chinese influence), but the ninth would be sought in vain by the well informed since it is in most cases concealed under the Bot.

The Viharn is bigger than the Bot and is that hall in which temple visitors bow to the ground three times before the statue of Buddha. Flower tributes, joss sticks and candles before, at times gilded, and always requiring veneration, Buddha – Thailand's ties with her religion are closest here. Especially lovely are the roofs, those very Thai roofs

The King feared for his position and for this reason he took as his wife the older sister of Mr. Stately, Shwe Myet Na, and made her Queen of the land. Miss Golden Face loved him very much. But in spite of this the King could find no peace and for this reason he told his wife to invite her brother to Court. When Mr. Stately arrived there, this led to his end. He was bound to a jasmin tree and burned on the King's orders. The Queen begged the King to allow her to say farewell to her brother – and she too leapt into the flames and perished. Too late the remorseful King ordered the flames to be put out.

Thus Mr. Stately and Miss Golden Face became ghosts. The most ancient of the 37 major Nats, the famed Magagiri-Nats. They took up their place in the jasmin tree and killed everyone who approached. Finally the Monarch ordered that the tree be felled and thrown into the Irrawaddy – the trunk drifted downstream and finally came to a rest caught in the rushes at Pagan.

The ghosts appeared to the Ruler of Pagan in a dream and related their sad tale, whereupon the Ruler had the two heads, still clearly seen in the tree, to be taken to a shrine on Popa as guards. Thereafter every King who came to power in Pagan had to make a pilgrimage to the two Nats "climb the Golden Mount" when he was crowned, this was an act as important as the coronation itself. Affairs of state were discussed with the two Magagiris, who had merged to become one, to become the "Lord of the Great Mountain".

And now back to reality as we know it. At the foot of the mount there is a monastery today in which once a year (May/June) the festival of spirits takes place. If a stranger wishes to visit the brother and sister he has to clamber halfway up the mount and then make the ascent to the peak via a steep stairway, where the statues of the two have found their last home in a spirit shrine.

whose origins are unknown and more typical of Thai architecture than anything else; this was once dismissed as confectioner's style, today one looks more closely.

Prang was built based on the style of the great Khmer. A tower like the Chedi which narrows towards the top, but not pointed, instead it is rounded off. A tower sanctuary of the Khmer then, which many experts attribute to southern Indian Viman. Thus making Prang a legacy of Hindu architecture. The best example is Wat Arun, a landmark in Bangkok.

Salas, small open-sided roofed over halls, invite temple visitors to rest, when, after the long approach, they have just passed the mighty Yaks, gigantic guard figures; smaller typical Chinese figures are found in many Wats, and in fact they do come from China. They made the long, hazardous, journey from China to Siam on rice junks as ballast.

Mondhop are found relatively rarely at Wats, which doesn't however lessen their significance. An education in elegant beauty is Wat Phra Buddha Badh

Prang

ferences, for instance in North Thailand, are also obvious. Nevertheless those features mentioned remain characteristic.

During the powerful Pagan Dynasty from the 11th to 14th centuries, industrious Buddhists built some 5,000 pagodas and temples. Why this tradition was maintained in a far from wealthy land such as Burma has a simple explanation; religious structures do not serve in purification or enlightenment of the masses, they serve improvement of the Karma of the builder; the more pagodas the better the karma. And this only applies to new buildings, restoration of existing buildings counts much less, something which is noticeable occasionally.

at Saraburi, the flightiest, and at the same time most impressive Mondhop structure in the country. Massive Nagas, mythological snakes, lie heavy on the balustrades of the ascent; their cobra-like heads blown up in a defensive position to fend off evil. Even when the name is taken from the Sanskrit mandapa = hall, the type is thoroughly Thai; the square layout of very often tiny halls under roofs one above the other finally ending in a peak. The Mondhop too has a specific purpose and accomodates important Buddhistic scripts, religious objects or – such as that at Saraburi – they crown a symbol of good fortune such as Buddhas's footprint.

Neither in Thailand nor Burma did the stilistic sense remain from the beginning to the present. New knowledge, outside influences, changed living conditions, all contributed to creation of variation in decoration which goes into great detail, and regional dif-

Mondhop

The Name of Perfection is Ananda –
Crown for a Temple

There is not much left of former might, Amiraddanapura, the "City that crushes its enemies" was the name borne by Pagan at the peak of its power. Dust has settled on the former greatness; the one time metropole of 500,000 inhabitants, in the hot, barren plains of the Irrawaddy, shrunk to a pitiful 3,000 souls, villagers. Between the 11th and 13th centuries when Pagan flourished and its rulers had temple after temple, pagoda after pagoda, stone after stone built to range into the blue Burmese skies, Pagan was the seat of a major power, Anawrahta was the name of the king who catapulted what had been a provincial town to the rank of a military power famed throughout all of South-east Asia.

I was right. You have to visit Pagan alone and on foot. Only then, with time to contemplate, with time to listen to the song of the cicadas in the almost unnatural stillness, with time to listen to the stillness, can you see the vision of mighty Pagan. Then the past rises not only out of the splendid temples but also out of the piles of rubble; artistically carved palaces of teak, richly decorated houses of the aristocracy, in between thousands of monks in saffron yellow robes, war elephants caparisoned in heavy red and yellow brocade, bustling courtiers – always ready to fulfil the slightest wish of the ruler – and slaves, the beasts of burden. Only the towering walls, which made Pagan almost unconquerable, set a limit to the visions.

And then you feel too the deep religiosity, understand the message of the temples and pagodas, know why here, where in truth nothing happens today, the heart of Burma still beats. For this was the cradle of Burmese culture; which was rocked in perfect timing by the gifted people of the Mon.

Mood makers: searing heat, that sets the horizon flimmering; I know that somewhere back there, there is the majestic Elephant River (Irrawaddy). Thistles, cacti, isolated palms, and lots of dust. No huts, although there are footpaths which seem to lead nowhere but must go somewhere. And amidst all this those 2,217 temples, pagodas and other holy buildings which haven't become ruins. Around 800 years ago it's said that these numbered 13,000, even more than at Angkor of the Khmer. A lonely ox-cart with the typical big wooden wheels and brightly coloured woven sides rumbles closer; an ox-cart stops: the driver with stained turban and teeth even more stained from betel takes me with him. My destination: Ananda Temple, petrified religion, triumph of the art of temple building.

Gentle contrast, when I finally get there, the white mass of Ananda gleams 51 metres (167 ft.) high out of the brown plain. This was the start of the Pagan's greatness; it was the same time their highpoint and harbinger of an early end; death and rebirth, no other structure in Pagan expresses this central theme of Buddhism more clearly than Ananda Temple; a temple that is more than perfect – it is perfection.

King Kyanzittha (1084–1112) must have had good, and some even better, days. On one of his best he gave the orders to build "Ananta panna", the eternal wisdom of Buddha was interpreted in stone by the master builders of the Mon in 1091; later the name became Ananda after one of Buddha's favourite students.

It is said that one day eight monks appeared before Kyanzittha's palace and told the ruler of a cave at the mountain Gandhamadana in which they had meditated; snow covered mountains rose up before Kyanzittha's mental eye – and the Ananda Temple was to be the earthly reality of this meditation. Mon builders could start their play with light.

For the temple is most impressive inside. The stone fretwork of the windows filters the light in geometric patterns; to provide an effective contrast with the exterior the impression was to be given of grottoes. This is once more a typical example of Mon style. And shafts too lead light in concentrated beams only to the upper section of the niches where the large figures are erected; almost 10 metres (32'10") above the illuminated faces of four Buddhas proclaim fleetingness of the last era of the world; Kakusandha in the niche facing North; Konagamana in that towards the East; Kassapa faces the South and finally Gautama towards the West; this last and Konagamana are copies, the originals were destroyed by temple robbers.

The niches were chiselled into the huge pillars that form the core of the temple. Around the centre two parallel walks which are connected with nar-

row corridors. These narrow, arched passages are clearly divided by two strips of windows, where the openings have been kept so small that the 80 flat reliefs showing scenes from Buddhas's life from birth to his enlightenment are wrapped in a mysterious twilight. Inscriptions in Mon give the names of the builders.

The roof, formed of five terraces narrowing towards the top, rises above the single storey lower section of Ananda and then becomes a Sikhara with a slender stupa crowned by a gold umbrella. The corners of the roof are decorated with smaller sikharas, the illusion of the snow capped mountain peak of the monks' cave legend is perfect. Miniature temples and guard lions as roof decorations take away some of the buildings's weightiness.

The Ananda Temple rises on a square plot with sides 88 metres long, and a surrounding wall turns the whole into holy ground. Gates mark four ascents, laid out for the four quarters of the heaven, whereby that at the North is best maintained and quite possibly the most important; they cross the two walks and only end at the temple's core, which results in a form resembling a classic Greek cross.

The temple is built of brick covered with plaster and in some places sandstone. At the western end there are still two of Budda's footprints with the traditional 108 symbolic signs and statues of King Kyanzittha and the monk Shin Arahan (see separate chapter) who introduced Hinayana-Buddhism under Anwarahta.

On the 8th of July 1975 Pagan suffered an earthquake which also badly shook Ananda Temple, that masterpiece of Mon architecture. The umbrella toppled and cracks appeared. Collections were made all over the country and donations given willingly for restoration of just this temple. The "crowning ceremony" was a festive occasion, when the umbrella (hti), weighing tons, was heaved with a winch into position, the Burmese proved once

more that although the greatness of Pagan has been history for centuries, sunk in the dust of the plains, Pagan lives on in the heart of the people.

Lost in thought I wander back to my hotel in the gentle light of the evening sun.

Art with Style

Thailand's geographical position as natural centre point of the South-east Asiatic region has had a major effect on art since time immemorial; many different trends flow together here. But in spite of these many influential factors, Thai art must be seen and understood as a separate entity.

A total of 8 periods in chronological sequence and areas represent development of art in Thailand in a somewhat inflexible scheme, whereby however a certain overlapping of periods and regions can't simply just be ignored. It is generally correct when one speaks of major differences in style among North Thailand (e.g. Chaingsaen), Central Thailand (Lopburi, Sukhothai) and the South.

The earliest period of Thai art is considered that of Dvaravati, which came into being in the 6th/7th centuries and reached its climax in the 7th/8th centuries; its influences were felt until into the 13th century. Statues of Buddha were the principle examples whereby certain influences of the Indian-Gupta period are also apparent. The greatest artistic achievement of this period were the prayer wheels such as is displayed by the exhibit dating from the 8th century at the museum in Bangkok. Structures, discovered from 1927 onwards,

were erected of brick made of unfired clay and they are accordingly in a sorry condition.

Already in the 8th century the Dvaravati Period diverted from that of Sri Vijayas – a Malayan kingdom which had its centre on Thai territory near Nakhon Si Thammarat on the Malayan Peninsula. An art direction which stems from Shivaism, Vishnuism as well as Mahayana-Buddhism, and which also displays elements of southern Indian, Indonesian, Khmer and Mon-Dvaravati influences.

Bodhisattvas dominate among the works of sculpture and many can be classified as masterpieces. This school also exerted major influence in continental Thailand until the 13th century in the field of architecture (decoration of temples with crenellations or miniature temples).

Between the 11th and 13th centuries Lopburi in Central Thailand became the most important outpost of the Cambodian Khmer and there unfolded in this area an art style which whilst bearing the imprint of Khmer influence, by no means adopted this type of artistic expression in a meaningless manner. True in Lopburi the style of Angkor

Art Periods

Thailand:

Dvaravati	6th/13th centuries, Buddha effigies, prayer wheels.
Sri Vijaya	8th/13th centuries, Bodhisattvas, architectural details.
Lopburi	11th/14th centuries, Bronzes, brick buildings, where available sandstone and laterite too.
Sukhothai	14/15th centuries, specific Buddha statues (striding Buddha), celadon ceramics.
Chiengsaen	13/19th centuries, Burmese influenced architecture.
U Thong	13th/15th centuries, elongated figures characteristic.
Ayutthaya	14th/18th centuries, "Golden Age" well defined Thai style with strong evidence of courtly variations.
Bangkok	19th/20th centuries, decorative elements, mannerism.

Burma:

Pyu	Up to 500 A.D. Indian stupa, flame arch ornamentation.
Mon	No art survived; from 11th century major builders in Pagan; Indian inspired cave temples with artistic lighting effects, square ground plan, Cella, peak as garnet (Orissa).
Birman	11th/13th centuries, rejection of earthly Mon style. 18th/19th centuries, renaissance of Mon style in Mandalay with stronger emphasis on decoration.

Wat (Phimai) was followed in architecture but for the most part building was carried out in brick and use was only made of sandstone, and later laterite, when the opportunity was provided through natural deposits. First class bronzes (e.g. figures of Buddha) tend towards Dvaravati style, Bodhisattvas are based on Khmer originals since here certain iconographical rules could not be broken. Around the middle of the 13th century a style took shape which was based on Indian Pala-iconography, which was later to influence the court art of Ayutthaya.

Ceylonese influences, more than any other, stimulated the art period of Sukhothai. The first great kingdom of the Thais only had one century to develop its own art on Thai territory; around the middle of the 15th century Sukhothai became dependent on Ayutthaya. However the Sukhothai Period, with its masterly effigies of Buddha, is considered the first really important period in Thai art; slender proportions, elegant postures, restrained inclination of the head and the first figure of Buddha striding forth. During this period Hinayana-Buddhism not only became rooted among the Thais (although Hindu influences were still maintained) a special feature was adopted on the exteriors of temples by way of celadon ceramics, which were designed based on Chinese examples. In as far as the buildings themselves were concerned, architects not only revised Khmer structures, they also incorporated influences of neighbouring peoples such as Indonesians and Burmese. Sukhothai's influence on subsequent developments in Thai art remains undisputed.

Pagan's influence on the other hand becomes apparent in the art of Chiengsaen in the field of architecture. The northern Thailand art period lasted from the end of the 13th century to the 19th century. In other words it still exerted influence even after the breakdown of the kingdom. Whilst sculptures in Chiangsaen followed the trend of Indian Pala, from the middle of the 15th century architecture went its own way. U Thong was the name of the princedom in Central Thailand where art reached its peak between the 13th and 15th centuries. The characteristic elongated figures were then reflected in the Ayutthaya Period.

The "Golden Age" of Thailand, the art period of Ayutthaya (14th–18th centuries) is divided into four sections. From the middle of the 14th century for some 100 years the art styles of Lopburi and Sukhothai determined that of Ayutthaya. Of significance to the second section was contact with Europe and the creation of a homogeneous ethnic style. From around 1630 not only the ancient Khmer traditions were decisive but there was also increasing adoption of European influences: from 1733 there was the fourth section which ended 34 years later with the destruction of Ayutthaya

by the Birmans. Whilst in sculpture and architecture old forms were maintained refined and with strong courtly components, the paintings of the time, well preserved even to the present, deserve special attention. And of course the many first class wood carvings which appeared at the same time, and the first brick palaces.

Many experts have decried the last Thai epoch, which was continued in Bangkok (Bangkok Period 19th/20th centuries) after the destruction of Ayutthaya, as confectioners' style. In the meantime however it is admitted that this enormously, decoratively emphasized art style is worthy of higher evaluation; European and Chinese influences are most apparent. Although at times sculptures, architecture and even paintings seem somewhat mannered.

Modern artists of today are attempting to adopt abstract styles; sculpting however has not until now followed the same path.

Art developments in Burma are less easy to define. In this case it was the various peoples, above all Pyu, Mon, Birman and Shan, who made their specific contribution to artistic development in the country. Throughout the history of art however Indian influences were more strongly adhered to than in Thailand; but nevertheless Burmese art also constitutes part of South-east Asian art as a whole, a framework into which she fits in spite of the Indian influences.

The most impressive testimonial of pre-Birman art in Burma are the 1,500 year old pagodas of the Pyu at Sri Ksetra. At the same time they are the oldest which have lasted until the present, at least as ruins; massive cones, some measuring up to 40 metres (131 ft.) in height, following Indian styles; detailed, well designed, effect arched ornaments over doors and windows, which are repeated again and again in the subsequent art of South-east Asia.

Purely Mon art, older than that of the Pyu, has not survived.

This great cultural people brought their skill as temple builders from Pagan. And Indian influences are not denied here either; ancient cave temples where latticed windows filter light in ghostly ornamentation in the inner temple; a Cella over a square ground plan under a terraced roof narrowing towards the top which soars heavenwards in the shape of a garnet. Orissa was the pattern. Later, from the 12th century on, the Burmese gave more expression to their own artistic feelings; light was the theme which they gave their temples, the cavelike character

was swept aside, the buildings lighter, more vital; the Pagoda builders loved the slenderer forms of the stupa – they were more ethereal, almost Gothic; the best example; the Shwe Dagon at Rangoon. And lightheartedness, as an escape from the darkness of the cave temples is manifested in the pyramidal roofs and the meditation halls. The Burmese sense of art contributed to clothing Indian art in the vital lightness of South-east Asia which also became almost lightheartedness.

Renaissance at the close of the period: Mandalay seat of the last Konbaung regents of Burma brought as revival of that Birman art which is to be seen as a symbiosis of Indian and South-east Asian; this revival however bore the stamp of decline, melancholy in graceful lightheartedness, just as prophesied by Buddhism; transition for a new existence.

Through Hell – at a Monastery

The scene: the Buddhist monastery Tham Krabok in central Thailand; the chain of hills, Prong Prab rises behind the flat buildings, giant trees provide protection from the sun. In the large hall of the main building, measuring 30 by 10 metres (98'5" by 32'10"), some 40 wasted figures lie on bamboo mats on the floor; official classification in the register, male. In a small side room a few women with 2 children, who make a somewhat frightened impression. All are apathetically withdrawn, no one has taken any notice of us; they seem exhausted. They all have something in common, they are opium addicts, and in the final stages of the illness. Tham Krabok; last gleam of hope for a way

out of this deadly habit. Method; medicinal plants. Buddhist monks have given permission for our visit.

Surat is just 40 and looks 60, he comes from the North of Thailand where opium cultivation is more profitable than anything else. Up there almost everyone has something to do with opium in one way or another. The lucky ones own a few acres of monsoon forest which they clear. And there are the carefully disguised opium fields against which the government in Bangkok is helpless. These families live well from the proceeds of raw opium, but for the most part they suck at the pipe, which promises sweet dreams, from childhood on; they are addicted.

Someone once said that opium addiction is death by installments. No one objected to this mad vicious circle. And when all is said and done these farmers in the North of Thailand are relatively fortunate. They went into the installment deal with death of their own free will.

It was otherwise for Surat – and representative for many. His parents numbered among the average countrywide; poor, with no land of their own. This doesn't mean too much as far as we are concerned, but in Thailand it can mean an insurmountable barrier to normal life. When Surat was six years old, he found out why; backbreaking work on strange rice fields; employer, what we would call, landed gentry.

Surat laboured, child labour is a normal fact of life, hardly any wages, instead a bowl of rice daily, sometimes vegetables or a minute piece of meat. He had to keep up his strength, that was the main thing. And when he reached 12 and has slaved for six years, for the first time a special ration; a tiny ball of pure opium with which Surat could escape his sad childhood in dreams.

Individual fate? Related without frills? "When in 1959 the government at long last passed the opium laws, there were 30 monks here", says the head of the monastery Tham Krabok, Soraijkassapa, "three years later we had treated more than 1,000 drug addicts". What is food for thought is that nothing was published by the monastery or the government in Bangkok about the withdrawal facilities at Tham Krabok.

Two things can be deduced from this; the number of opium addicts is high in Thailand; but there are many among them who wish to break out of

Opium is prepared from the juice of the opium poppy (Papaver somniferum). The unripe capsule of the poppy is slit and the milky juice which seeps out is allowed to dry in the air and then removed, as raw opium.

Opium contains 25 different alkaloids (among them morphine and codeine) and has for years been used as a sedative in medicine. Also taken as a stimulant and narcotic, misuse of the drug leads to addiction.

the vicious circle if the necessary help is not refused. Addiction is widespread above all among the mountain people.

Neun Tudong, an ascetic wandering monk of Hinayana-Buddhism, withdrew to a cave near the present monastery in 1957. He devoted himself to meditation which he attempted to intensify

139

with plant drugs. It was almost by chance that in this way a possible means was found to combat opium addiction. When two years later the first sentences were passed by Thai courts for drug abuse, many found the only help among the community of monks at the monastery which in the meantime had grown to number 30.

"At the time we were still in the experimental stage, we know very little about any cures" this is how a monk described the situation. But only three years later the courageous monks, had perfected their fight against drugs with medicinal plants to such an extent, that even Bangkok sat up and took notice. The country spared no expense; the monks were given land and financial support in order to build the monastery as it stands today. The only condition attached to the support, which has remained an isolated instance to date, that the drug addicts had to be treated free of charge as in the past. The "Central Security Division" responsible for the war on drugs in Bangkok, grasped the opportunity and sent the ailing to Tham Krabok.

The balance is imposing; in the twenty years since the start of the project (1963) more than 60,000 patients have been treated; some 70% could be discharged as cured, 25% suffered relapses and the remaining 5% are hopeless cases where treatment was broken off.

The only recognition to date; in 1979 the community received the Magsaysay Award, named after the former president of the Philippines and a kind of Asian Nobel Prize. If one remembers that the figure for successful cures is in our countries some two thirds less, then the award simply has to be regarded as more than well earned.

Treatment at Tham Krabok is voluntary. Men and women, and lately foreigners too, gather what remains of their strength and will to reach the monastery office, unsuspecting that before them lie two weeks of pure hell. They have to surrender all their possessions when entering the monastery; then they are stripped. All are issued the same red shorts and white T-shirts. A monk then shows the new arrivals to their sleeping mats, rooms for men and women are separate. After some information on Tham Krabok and the type of treatment, Buddha's help is begged for with the aid of Sa-a, a tribute.

So far, so good. After the first evening the novice drinks a glass of plant juices. Around five minutes later there then begins what the suffering graphically described as "the devil leaving the body"; they kneel in long rows in the monastery courtyard, and shaking with severe cramps, vomit continuously, throwing up violent fountains of the tincture. This is intended to rid the body of drugs. In the background the monks murmur prayers.

"Our unbelievable success, by far the highest we know is not based primarily on medical treatment", a monk states, "at least 80% of our success is undoubtable due to the religious-psychological treatment and only the remaining 20% is due to the medicinal plants".
More than 100 plants form the basis of the brew which the patients receive punctually at 9.30 a.m. for the first 10 days of treatment, and sometimes it is administered with force. For who ever has declared himself ready to take this drastic cure, is not allowed to draw out, may not break it off.

As far as the plants themselves are concerned it is only known that they are gathered in the immediate vicinity

Red Juice – Not Always Blood

The old man's lip are dark red, his teeth almost black. Dozens of red stains on the hard packed ground around his hut in the small village in Upper Burma near Mandalay. They look like blood. But in Thailand and Burma red juice is rarely blood, for the most part the Betel chewers have left their trade mark.

Chewing the stimulating betel nut of the palm of the same name (botanic name Areca Palm) ist widespread in Asia and the Pacific; Thailand and Burma are no exceptions. Nevertheless the number of betel chewers is decreasing rapidly. Young people don't regard the dark red lips and black teeth a symbol of beauty any more, and these can't be avoided after years of chewing the nuts.

The practice is said to act as a stimulant and it also suppresses any feelings of hunger. The taste is terrible. The bitter juice which results from chewing is spat out as quickly as possible otherwise an upset stomach is the result.

It is older people who are for the most part addicted, it is cheap because the ingredients are supplied by nature, small pieces of nut are wrapped in betel leaves with ground lime and the stimulating alkaloid set free by chewing. The saliva is coloured red by the dye of the unripe nut. And experts then skilfully spit out the juice. At one time the offer of betel was a sign of hospitality and some researchers even see in it a concealed sexual symbol. The fatal consequences: after years of chewing severe inflammation can occur in the mouth, and even lead to cancer of the mouth or tongue.

Seen from this point of view it's not always a bad thing when old customs die out. The older Burmese however will never give up chewing betel, which is somewhat similar to dependency on nicotine.

---

of the monastery for the most part, some 20% are gathered by monks all over Thailand. Some herbs are dried and ground, and then mixed with the juices extracted from others. The liquid is then boiled. The patient swallows 30 cubic centimetres of the mixture each day. This results in such a violent revolt on the part of the body that severe cramps occur.

On the second day of treatment hysterical outbursts are frequent, and at times attempted escapes because the treatment is almost brutally intensified. Steam baths are given in addition to the plant juices, which contain similar herbs. Fevers or muscular cramps which occur are handled without ado with cold showers; occasionally tonics to build up strength are administered as well.

The medical treatment is accompanied by a ten day psycho-programme with strong religious overtones. This includes meditation, prayer and tributes. Discussions take place with the monks on the social causes for drug consumption and the future life without addiction is outlined. General opinion is that these talks are of great value. And in addition light work, with musical entertainment between, is intended to restore some of the patient's mental and physical strength.

Many patients express the wish to remain in the monastery for a time after completion of treatment, a wish which is granted to almost one half; there are no costs since Tham Krabok is supported by donations from the people. During this period of rehabilitation there is no further medical treatment and the patient has the opportunity for vocational training. New agricultural methods, hygiene – above all for women – take the forefront. And many a patient who previously wasn't in a position to even ride a bike, can afterwards skillfully drive the monastery tractor.

At the time of our visit 54 men and women were in treatment at the monastery Tham Krabok. They had all reached the end of the road as far as opium addiction is concerned. The youngest patient celebrated his fourth birthday; he had been born an addict.

Gay Charm – The Festivals

Santa Claus, or at least the Burmese version, visits the good children there too. His name is Thagyarmin, and he ist highest ranking of the 37 Burmese Nats, King of all Heavenly spirits, and probably has his origins in Hindu mythology. But in the same way as St. Nicholas, as known on the European continent, he rewards the good and punishes the naughty. He comes riding on a golden Pegasus and carries a water urn, symbol of peace and prosperity. Everyone looks forward to the arrival of Tha-gyarmin, or Sakkra as he is sometimes called; tubs full of water are placed in readiness.

Tourists who are a little water shy should keep a distance between themselves and Thailand and Burma in the middle of April each year. For then, on a day calculated exactly by the astrologers, the Buddhist New Year is celebrated. Three days before the actual date forecast there are high spirited water fights in the villages and towns. "Thinjan" ist the name the Burmese have for this festival, which is called "Songkran" by the Thais.

The purpose behind this damp frolic? Body and – symbolically – soul are purified and go thus into the New Year. On the morning of New Year's Day the people make a pilgrimage to statues of Buddha which they symbolically sprinkle with water. Relatives are visited and monks especially extravagantly served. And Tha-gyarmin comes to the children. In Thailand it is also believed that rainfall depends on the amount of water sprayed, the more water, the better the rainfall and the better the harvests.

Interest in purity of the spirit also leads the Thais to generously spraying strangers too; so any cold shower taken in this way should be greeted with a smile even when it appears that the small boys are more interested in seeing the farangs (= strangers) dripping wet than they are in the purity of their souls!

As in so many other things in this fairytale country, a fairytale also forms the background of Singkran, and makes it more appealing to the eye. A god, so the story goes, lost a bet with a human and for this reason had to behead himself. Pretty girls form a procession, as water nymphs, in which the head of the unfortunate god is borne aloft by one of his seven daughters. The water festival is particularly high spirited at Chiang Mai.

Less light-hearted are the Festivals of Lights. The Burmese celebrate two of these, and the first in October/November heralds the start of the most beautiful time of year – and at the same time the best time for marriage. Buddha had risen to Heaven to bring his message to the gods and spirits – including his

mother – living there. When he returned to earth it was night, believers lit thousands of lights to guide the Enligtened One safely back to earth. Today this festival marks the end of the Buddhist fasting time. Lanterns are hung out and candles lit.

Tassaung Daing, the second Burmese Festival of Light which is celebrated when the moon is full at the end of November, puts the skill and speed of the weavers in the right light. There are competitions among the nimble fingered girls and the one who has completed a certain part of a monk's robe first is the winner. They are also at work at the Shwe Dagon Pagoda of Rangoon. Those monks who leave the monastery after the fast are made a gift of the robes.

Tod Kathin is the name the Thais have for this festival when the monks can look forward to new robes. The traditional procession of the Royal Barges, which was at one time a highpoint, no longer takes place today. Something which is to be regretted.

Thousands of decorated, illuminated, boats shaped in the form of lotus blossoms from banana leaves throng the rivers of Thailand. These krathong – as they are called – are loaded with flowers and coins and drift as a symbolic gift on the lifegiving Mother Water to the sea. Loi Krathong is the name of this celebration which takes place in the 12th Lunar month (November) mainly at Chiang Mai.

By the way the Thais must be about the only people on earth in the happy position of celebrating New Year three times a year. Since the change was made to the Gregorian calender, officially New Year is on the 1st of January. Around one month later there follows the spectacular Chinese New Year celebrations. And finally, around the middle of April, that of the Buddhists.

The highest religious holiday in Thailand is still Visakha Buja. On the first day of the full moon in May the Buddhists commemorate the birth, enlightenment and passing of Buddha into Nirvana. In illuminated, decorated, monasteries, the faithful, carrying home-made lanterns, make a circuit three times of the main shrine. The same festival is known in Burma where it is called Nyaung Ye. Ceremoniously, flower-decked girls pour water over the Bodhi trees (Ficus religiosa) in the pagoda grounds; and special care is taken to ensure that roots of this tree, which is holy in Buddhism, are generously watered and thus ensure that the doctrine flourishes, symbolically of course.

In Burma however even Buddha pays a visit, in a festival bursting with religious joy. At the time of the full moon in the month Wagaung (July/August) the monks are offered a meal. A large basket is set up to take the notes bearing the name of each monk of the village community. One of these bears the name Buddha. These notes are drawn in the same way as lots and that monk whose name is drawn is invited to a feast on the following day.

More spectacular from a visual aspect is the Karaweik Festival at the Inle Lake of the Shan state. This starts at the lakeside pagoda of Phaung Daw U, the pagoda of the "Royal Barges". Four holy statues of Buddha are borne by these majestic, richly decorated, barges to the 13 villages of the lake, as a sign of blessing. An impressive scene: the famous leg rudderers of the Inthas, sheltered by splendid umbrellas, guide these ceremonial barges over the lake.

Anyone travelling in Burma in the month of Nadaw (November/December) has the opportunity of experiencing one of the many Nat festivals. In honour of a special spirit, always responsible for a specific village, the inhabitants perform the trance dance and ceremonies. This is intended to symbolize the trance dancer being possessed by the Nat who makes contact with the villagers through the medium. Other major Nat festivals – such as that of Mount Popa – the so-called Nayon Celebrations – can also be on the calender of festivals at other times of the year.

In the heart of Bangkok, at Phramane Square, the starting signal is given for a very special event in April/May. A Royal Ploughing Ceremony. The day and hour are forecast by the Court Astrologer and mark the beginning of ploughing for the rice farmers of Thailand. The Royal pair, priests, astrologers, princesses and white oxen are the leading characters. These flower decorated bulls draw a holy plough which turns a few furrows in the grass of Phramane Square. Musicians, umbrella bearers and "heavenly" maids, carrying rice seeds in holy vessels, follow. Then a tray is brought from the royal tribune with seven silver vessels filled with grain and herbs, water and wine; the animals are led to these to feed and whatever they eat or drink is said to be abundant in the following year.

Just before this however, at this central square, the fight takes place between Chula and Pakpao; Chula is male, Pakpao the female – both are dragon kites flown by skilled hands. The male dragon, up to 2 metres (6'7") long, carries a bamboo hook to catch as many of the much smaller Pakpaos

The Burmese harp has fourteen silk-strings.

as possible, and pull them into his territory; occasionally the proud Chula however also takes a fall.

The list of official, non-religious, holidays in Thailand and Burma is on the long side. The people work hard, and take pleasure in celebrating.

Thailand's Chakri Day on the 6th of April celebrates the foundation of the present dynasty and is a national holiday, the people do honour to the ruling and past monarchs at the hall of the Emerald Buddha with flowers and joss sticks. On the 5th of May the coronation of King Bhumipol is celebrated, and the 12th of August is Queen Sirikit's birthday; on this day she makes gifts to the monks at Chitralada Palace. On the 5th of December Bangkok puts on festive dress: coloured lights, flags – and portraits of the King everywhere, mark his birthday. Before this, on the

23rd of October, mountains of flowers at the memorial to King Chulalongkorn, the important 5th ruler of the Chakri Dynasty, this is the anniversary of his death.

More democratic, as we see it and therefore less royal, are the official holidays in Burma. The 4th of January is on the list as Independence Day since on this day Burma left the British Commonwealth of Nations and achieved independence. On February 12th the many ethnic groups of the land are reminded of national loyalties on the "Day of Unity"; on this day in 1947 the national hero Aung San signed at Pangkong a national agreement with representatives of the minorities.

Socialism is celebrated on the 2nd of March as "Day of the Farmers" and on May 1st as "Workers Day". Events on 27th March are more of a military nature when "Resistance Day" is celebrated with parades to mark resistance to Japanese occupation during World War II. Since the 19th of July 1947, that day on which Aung San was assassinated with six of his ministers and closest workers, this day is solemnly remembered as "Martyrs' Day".

The calender of holidays in Thailand and Burma is based on phases of the moon, which means that those festivities stemming from Buddhism, or in any way connected with this, fall on a different day each year, so that no firm dates can be given. In keeping with the national character of both countries, festival are, for the most part, gay and dominated by good cheer. A Burmese proverb says that the need to laugh is greater than that to cry. Charming gaiety, given expression in celebrations.

Entertainment

Let's be brief. Anyone looking for only entertainment, or at least some kind of diversion, will be disappointed in Burma. Even in the cities the shutters are down by 9 p.m. There are no bars, hardly any public restaurants, and entertainment – if at all – is only offered at the few big hotels; and films too are rare. Street theatre (pwe) in Rangoon and Nat ceremonies in Mandalay are not organised and seen by chance. The only exception: the Karaweik Restaurant in Rangoon not only offers good meals in the evening but also Burmese traditional dances, and not especially devised for the tourists either.

Possibilities for entertainment in Thailand are almost unlimited. There's any number of first class restaurants in all towns (don't be put off by the outside), which do full justice to Thai cuisine. Thai classic dance and shows by the mountain tribes of the North are anyway always on every tourists itinerary. For those with dancing on their minds, but not exactly the traditional kind, Bangkok has plenty to offer; bars with Go Go girls line whole streets (for instance Patpong or Soi Cowboy). Tips are passed on by word of mouth. Theatre shows and films round off the entertainment programme.

No matter how you spend your evenings in Thailand, it doesn't cost a fortune, and there's something for all tastes. But, don't make the mistake of carrying all your money on you, for some it would mean the first, and last, night on the town. If you want to put on your dancing shoes yourself, the hotel discos are best, but then of course it is just that little bit more expensive.

Eating, Drinking

Gourmets insist that Thailand's cuisine is the best of all. And there is a Thai proverb which puts the variety offered by these past masters of the "Land of the Free" into the right (restaurant) limelight: 365 times a year the Thais can choose among different lunches and evening meals. People from other countries where seasonings are not used with quite such abandon, do have to become accustomed to some "hot", in all senses of the word, dishes.

Everything that can creep, fly, swim or run lands in the Thai pot; they're not at all finicky. Sauces and spices change the "raw materials" so much that it's often difficult to say what these were anyway...

Rice ist the basic ingredient of all, or nearly all dishes. Vegetables are used by the Thai cook so cunningly and in such variety that even the most familiar sorts assume an astonishing and unusual delicacy of taste: plus the fact that chili sauce stands on all restaurant tables and now and again the thought does arise that this might just be a way to promote sales of drinks; but the spiciness can't even be lessened with the good Thai beer, which is considered a luxury and expensive accordingly.

Speciality from Sukhothai, which no one should miss: Winged beetles are attracted by lights and caught during the night; truly spicy beetles, crushed and mixed into a sauce. Another speciality which is perhaps more to our taste is Dimsum; little envelopes made of rice flour dough filled with ground meat and vegetables and fried in oil or simmered in meat broth.

At all events it would be a little like taking coals to Newcastle, as the English saying goes, to ask for Chinese or European dishes or dishes of any other country in Thailand; you really should let yourself in for the pleasant adventure of Thai skill with food.

Less adventurous is Burma, lack of supplies being the main reason. Certainly Burmese culinary skills are worthy of respect, it's just that the variety is very much less. Spiciness ist also popular in Burma, but the Thai are more imaginative. Various fish pastes, curry and rice are the basic items on the menu; plus of course fruit and beef, poultry and pork. Even today the Buddhist influence is so strong that Moslem Pakistanis have to be hired as butchers since the Burmese are not allowed to kill animals. Eating meat and drinking alcohol was in the past punishable with death. Today attitudes are more liberal although the only beer available, "Mandalay Beer" ist so low in alcohol content it probably wouldn't even offend an abstainer.

And a word about drinks in Thailand: "Mekong" whisky which is distilled with rice, is offered cheaply as the national drink. Spoiled palates won't, at least at first, find this much to their taste, later it seems people get so accustomed to it that frequently bottles of "Mekong" are seen poking out of the corners of some baggage. Highly recommended – especially at lunch time – 2 fingers of Mekong with a good shot of soda water and the juice of two limes, it's a refreshing drink, tastes pleasant, and doesn't give you a – when drunk in moderation – thick head.

Shopping

At the airport at Bangkok it becomes clear that Thailand is a shopper's paradise. Excess baggage is the order of the day. And the same thing applies to Burma.

Both countries offer the tourist goods in quantities and qualities which are hard to beat. Shopping is encouraged in a big way so much so that many a wallet shrinks to hold only as much as is absolutely necessary.

Lacquered Ware from souvenirs costing very little, to really valuable masterpieces are offered by some 1,000 makers in the Burmese Pagan area; in Thailand Chiang Mai is the main place for lacquer.

Chinese Porcelain, also celadon, has become a much sought after souvenir; Burma's temples, and the Diplomatic Store, 143–144 Sule Pagoda Road, Rangoon, are treasure troves. The best address in Thailand is said to be Celadon House, 278 Silom Road, Bangkok. Chinese craftsmen brought the art of porcelain making to Thailand in the 14th century.

Marionettes: in traditional costumes, which were also used in shows, could best be bought to date in the small shops at the approach to the Mahamuni (Arakan) Pagoda in Mandalay;

pretty bronze work and wood carvings are also found here. Burmese puppets are becoming more and more popular with tourists.

A "bestseller" has been for ages now Burmese "Opium Weights" which the connoisseur doesn't buy as single pieces, but in sets ranging from a few grams up. Old opium pipes have on the other hand become rare but with some luck they can still sometimes be found either in Pagan or at the Inle Lake.

The Inthas by the way reached some affluence as a result of their **weaving skills** and lovely materials can be bought also around the area of Inle Lake.

The workshops in Mandalay and surrounding villages are well known for **ivory crafts.** But care should be taken that ivory carvings can be imported into your country; some countries have strict rules on the protection of threatened species and ban imports.

Opportunities for shopping are even greater in Thailand than in Burma. In addition to the celadon and lacquer already mentioned, the main attraction is **silk.** But remember the best silks are not bought in Bangkok but instead Chiang Mai. A whole industry has been built up there around silk. And **cotton** too is worth looking at because of the pretty, tasteful patterns.

What has to be borne in mind as far as articles of **bronze** or **silver** are concerned is that antiques may only be taken out of the country when permission is granted by the "Fine Arts Department". There's a general ban on export of Buddha's whether old or new.

Whilst in Burma it's best to resist the temptation to buy **precious stones,** Bangkok is still reasonable and also a major source. A great deal of valuable rubies, sapphires and jade comes from Burma and reaches Thailand by way of mysterious smugglers routes. Buying should only be done at reputable shops in Bangkok and a certificate testifying to the genuine article asked for; the danger that you could buy a lemon, as the saying goes, is considerable.

Masks (Khon Dance) make attractive wall decorations and are comparably reasonable in price.

Undisputed centre of **wood carving** in Thailand is still Chiang Mai; the choice is vast and ranges from small figures to complete suites of furniture, which reach the buyer by sea after a few weeks or months. Old wood carvings (Buddhas mainly) are best bought at the antique dealers in this town. Most of these, some very valuable, **antiques** come from Burma and were smuggled into Thailand. The shop owners send the wood carvings as teak wood by air, and get round the export ban this way.

Ivory carvings can also be bought in Thailand but the same applies as in Burma.

Bargaining is in, in Thailand and Burma. There are shops and stores in Bangkok and Chiang Mai which have recently introduced "fixed prices" but even these are prepared to give a discount if the order is good enough. The rule of thumb is: bargain one third off the price asked. Bargaining is not considered ill-mannered or a sign of shortage of money in either country; quite the opposite: a determined haggler actually earns respect. Anyone wishing to be absolutely sure can make use of the "Official Shopping Guide", a list of stores drawn up by the Thai tourist organisation which can be got at the tourist offices or hotels.

Many stays in Thailand end with flowers, wonderful arrangements of **orchids** have become almost a standard, even if short-lived souvenir. They are beautiful and cheap and, for as long as they last, the memory of what, one hopes, was an unforgettable experience remains.

Tourist's Bangkok

A city that provokes contradiction; and is a contradiction. Bangkok – for those with an eye on Asia of the last century – the very epitomy of exotic appeal; temples stretching golden peaks into the blue skies, gliding in slender boats on the canals past picturesque houses on piles covered in climbing orchids. For those standing in the reality of Silom Road, Bangkok is above all noisy, hectic and the air is not heavy with the perfume of tropical blossoms, but stinks of exhaust fumes.

The truth about Bangkok, if there is such a thing, lies somewhere between, lies in subjective experience.

Objective nevertheless are the temples in almost lighthearted beauty; museums stuffed full with, sometimes beautiful, and always important, testimonies of the past; markets, bursting with life like a ripe papaya; quaintly unique places like the Thieves Market or goose-pimpling unique like the Snake Farm; a few remaining Khlongs, where loud outboard motors chatter; a night life that leaves nothing to wish for and sometimes stirs up an indescribable longing; shopping centres with goods from all corners of the earth; and finally the dignified and honoured relics of the dynastic order of things, such as the Royal Barges.

And all this unrestrainedly youthful, for Bangkok is only 200 years old; a youth on clay feet however – Bangkok is sinking deeper into the mud every year.

Taking the lead, in the older part of the city, **Wat Phra Keo,** which actually is called Wat Phra Sriratana Sasdaram. Within the precincts of the Royal Palace, which because of an absolute lack of style becomes of more once worth

seeing, the royal Wat in purely Thai architectural style asserts itself against all outside influences of earlier periods. Earlier Indian, Chinese and Cambodian influences were apparent, also at Wat Phra Keo for instance.

This "Emerald Buddha Temple", as Wat Phra Keo is also called first took shape in 1784/85. Rama I, as the founder of the Chakri Dynasty, still royal familiy today, had two years previously moved the capital of the new kingdom from Thonburi, capital after the destruction of Ayutthaya, to the other side of the river. As the leader of his people, also in a religious sense, he needed a truly royal temple. And Wat Phra Keo became just that. It is not only the highpoint of every sightseeing tour of the city, it is also a tourist magnet in a special class of its own.

The "Emerald Buddha Temple", which never included accomodation for the monks because it lies in the palace grounds, has been thoroughly renovated twice in recent times; once in 1957 to celebrate 2,500 years of Buddhism, and in 1981 just before the 200th anniversary of the founding of Bangkok. Since then Wat Phra Keo scintillates in new brilliance, a brilliance which just misses being overpowering.

On an area of some 3,000 square metres (4.45 ac.), a tenth of the total palace grounds, there rise within a surrounding wall, various buildings which vary as to function and layout. Six gates, each flanked by **Yaks** (guards) six metres (19'8″) high, enclose the hallowed area. These 12 figures all have different, but always terrifying grimacing faces and wear different costumes.

Scenes from the ancient Indian epos Ramayana, called Ramakien in Thailand, decorate the covered walks, which traverse the **inside of the surrounding walls.** The story of the noble, suffering, love between Rama and Sita is brought graphically and realistically to life in the eyes of the wondering public. The Ramayana is considered, with the Mahabharata also from India, the longest epic poem in the world and even today exercies influence throughout all of South-east Asia as an example and education that marital love and faithfulness triumphs in the end in spite of all obstacles.

Large and monumental at the same time ist the Bot. This building which is only reached after passing the main portal is the most important of all. Inside, some 11 metres (36 ft) above the marble floor, on a richly decorated plinth, the 66 cm (2'2") Emerald Buddha has been erected; which by the way is not of emerald but in fact green jade. The effigy is considered the symbol of royalty of the Chakri Dynasty and the King carries out holy rites here: three times a year (since Rama III, previously only twice yearly) at the start of the dry season, the start of the hot season and the start of the rainy season, the Monarch changes the figure's robes.

The relatively small Buddha looks back on a great and changeable past. Records mention the figure for the first time in 1436, but it is more than likely that the figure was already carved in north Thailand in the 13th century. It is said to have been erected in a Chedi at Chiang Rai, covered in plaster and gold leaf. During transportation the covering cracked open and exposed the nephrite stone. Then, according to ancient sources the ruler of Chiang Mai hat the Emerald Buddha brought to Lampang and finally to Chiang Mai. When this capital of the North was captured by Laos (1551) the Buddha was taken to

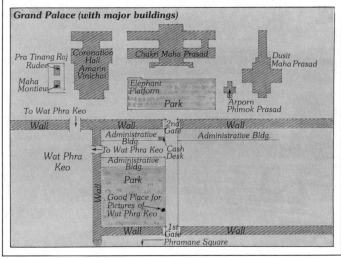

Grand Palace (with major buildings)

Luang Prabang and a few years later to Vientiane, the new capital. Finally under King Taksin, who so successfully led the remains of the Ayutthaya army defeated by the Burmese. Laos was defeated and General Chakri, later Rama I, bore the statue in triumph to Thonburi; it was to find its final home at Wat Phra Keo in Bangkok.

Above the figure as a sign of its importance nine umbrellas and crystal spheres symbolising sun and moon, before the pedestal a Buddha sculpture donated by King Mongkut. At both sides Buddhas in royal robes hold gilded, ceremonial umbrellas; Rama III had dedicated these to his predecessor. Trees of gold and silver and gifts complete the picture inside the Bot.

The red-gold sheen of the Bot's ceiling reflects on the wall paintings depicting scenes of important events in Buddha's life. In between, painted with the same care, scenes from the 550 Jatakas, Buddha's former lives. Below these are graphic presentations of Siamese warriors from the time of the first Chakri Dynasty.

Shoes, strictly forbidden inside, can be put on again after leaving the Bot. Now attention turns to the twelve **Salas,** shadowy resting places and the eight **Bai Semas,** which surround the Bot. These magical stones, symbols of the holiness of the building, separate it from the surrounding temple buildings. The hallowed area is also surrounded by a balustrade and pairs of bronze lions guard the four gates to the square structure with so typical Thai roof. The carved eaves show the Hindu god Vishnu on his pack animal, the sun eagle Garuda. This Garuda at the same time heraldic animal of the land, is repeated 112 times, holding the Naga snake, on the outside walls of the Bot; then there are mother-of-pearl decorations and plaster work in blue-gold with

which the Thai architects have lent the building an atmosphere of lightness.

On a wide marble terrace, raised above the level of the remaining area and north of the Bot, several buildings; the Royal Pantheon, the library and finally a golden Stupa, built at the command of Rama IV. High gabled roofs, the yellow centre tower, soaring as a Prang, with the crown on its "spire", make the Pantheon, the **Prasad Phra Tebhidorn,** unmistakable. This building, which is only open to the public once a year on Chakri Day, 6th April, was built in 1885 in the form of a Greek cross and completely restored in 1903. It houses life-size statues of the first eight kings of the Chakri Dynasty. At the stairway gilded statues of mythological creatures among them the famous Kinnari and Kinnara, half bird half man or woman.

Close to the statues of holy white elephants, found during the reign of the first Chakri kings, is the **Maha Mandapa** (Mondhop), the library. With its square shape, surrounding pillared gallery and pointed roof this building displays all the classic features of a Mondhop. The wooden structure is decorated with gilded carvings and glass mosaics, inside – no admission – it houses the Buddhistic Tripitaka recorded in Thai and Pali; this is the written record of Therawada Buddhism. A floor of silver slabs and gold ornamented walls lend the inner room special dignity.

Right next door the soaring **Chedi,** the Golden Pagoda at the eastern part of the terrace; its tiles make it the brilliant focal point of the temple area. Four doors, kept closed at all times, lead to a small tower inside in which a Buddhistic relic is said to be walled in. In 1885 King Chulalongkorn had the Golden Pagoda built over this small tower.

And next to the Mondhop; a monument to a victory. Just here King Mongkut had a model of the magnificent temple of Angkor Wat erected, since also during his reign Cambodia was a vassal state of Siam without a trace of its earlier power; and today the five towers of Angkor Wat can be admired in miniature at least.

Finally there is a third group of buildings below the terrace on a level with the Bot, and the west front of the **Hor Monthien Dam** (a second library) is worth a close look; it is considered the most beautiful in all Thailand. The inlaid mother-of-pearl work of the doors stems from Ayutthaya and number among the few art treasures which survived the destructive Burmese attacks. Holy Buddhist scriptures are also kept in Hor Monthien Dam.

More sober on the other hand is Vihan Yot, opposite the second library with its crown-like tower. This prayer hall contains the Mananga Sila, a stone slab which served the Sukhothai King Ram Kamheng as a throne. King Mongkut found the stones, during the period he spent with a religious order, when excavating at the ruins of Sukhothai and had them brought to Bangkok. Porcelain and ceramic works decorate the outside walls of Vihan Yot and the inlaid mother-of-pearl on the doors is also worth seeing.

Phra Nak the last building in the north-west corner of the temple grounds serves as a mausoleum, the urns containing the ashes of members of the Chakri Royal Family are kept here; Phra Nak is also characterised by a telescope style roof.

Eight **Prangs,** two inside the temple walls and six outside, rise in a row along the east gallery and symbolize either the eight planets known in earlier times or Buddha, the doctrine, the community, the disciples, the monks, the King, pre-Buddha and future Buddhas. These are decorated with ceramic tiles and mirror mosaic.

Special attention is deserved for **a small statue** which receives flower tributes from the faithful more frequently than any other at Wat Phra Keo. This is at the west front of the Bot housing the Emerald Buddha and is considered a memorial to an Indian hermit who worked as a doctor in Thailand. The cylindrically shaped stone in front of the memorial is said to be the pestle which he used in making his medicines. Opposite this, at the south-east corner, another small structure with coloured tiles, the contents of which become important at the annual ceremony of ploughing held at Phramane Square, the **Hor Phra Kantaraj** houses a Buddha effigy honoured as the weather god and is carried to the ceremony.

Admission to Wat Phra Keo ist free on Sundays and public holidays, other days admission is charged.

Much less impressive than the temple buildings is the **Grand Palace,** which has today lost a great deal of its former importance. Whilst Wat Phra Keo expresses clearly Thai style, the palace bears the unmistakable imprint, in some sections, of European influence.

The Grand Palace occupies part of the grounds on which Wat Phra Keo stands. Rama I had building started in 1782/83 and since then almost every ruler has made additions or changes, for this reason it's hardly surprising that the architecture shows styles which range from Thai to Rennaissance. On Tuesdays and Thursdays from 9 a.m. to 4 p.m. and on Mondays, Wednesdays and Fridays from 9 a.m. to 12 noon, the palace can be viewed – shorts on either sex are forbidden, men have to roll down shirt sleeves, and headgear has to be removed.

The main entrance is on **Phramane Square** which is also called Royal Square (Sanam Luang). This square is thought to be the historic centre point of Bangkok and the most interesting buildings are found in the immediate vicinity. It is here that ceremonial cremation takes place as well as the festival of the first ploughing, but the square becomes a meeting place for the city's inhabitants above all on Saturday and Sunday when the big week-end market flourishes. When the South wind blows however the dragons take over; then the male and female dragons rise, in the popular combat, into the blue skies above Thailand.

The palace itself had served its purpose as a location for political decisions by 1946 at latest. At that time King Ananda died under circumstances which haven't been fully explained to the present day and King Rama IX. Bhumipol, as his sucessor, moved to the more modern Chitralada Palace. Now, however, the Grand Palace is only a showpiece for state banquettes and other political receptions.

Relatively uninteresting administrative buildings line both sides of the inner gate and then the way is free to **Chakri Maha Prasad.** English architects planned this huge Audience Room which was built in 1876 during the reign of King Rama V. The roof is pure Thai in style whereas the remainder can be said to have been strongly influenced by Renaissance styles.

Chakri Maha Prasad also houses the Throne Room with its splendid crystal chandeliers; nine-tiered white umbrella is raised over the Niel Throne as a symbol of the King. Historic paintings decorate the Throne Room, which by the way is not open to the public.

The hall to the right of Chakri Maha Prasad is worthy of more attention. **Dusit Maha Prasad** its name, and it is one of the oldest buildings in the palace grounds. This "State Room" was erected on the orders of Rama I already in 1783 as a Coronation Room, in the form of a Greek cross. The tiered roofs end in a Mondhop, especially lovely are the carved teak, gilded, gables, the decorated roof supports and the exquisitely designed window frames. Four large depictions of the sun eagle Garuda decorate the base of the Mondhop. Garuda as pack animal of Fishnu has his origins in the pantheon of Hindu gods, but as one of Vishnu's incarnations, the tenth, was Buddha. Hindu mythology also has its place in Buddhism.

After the death of Rama I solemn death rites took place in Dusit Maha Prasad before the body was cremated at Phramane Square and since then this hall has served for the death ceremonies before the cremation of a Chakri King. Crowning ceremonies on the other hand are no longer held here. A series of small Garuda figures support a gold throne at one side of the building, where Rama I received the emissaries of his subject countries. The inside walls of the main building, blue and gold, are ornamented with leaves and vines and angels rising out of lotus blossoms. A black throne decorated with mother-of-pearl, stands under a nine-tiered umbrella and the extravagant bed of Rama I can also be seen here.

Directly in front of the Dusit Maha Prasad is a small attractive pavilion, **Arporn Phimok Prasad,** which was used as a model for the Thai Pavilion at the World Exhibition at Brussels. King Mongkut had this "loveliest of all pavilions" as it is called, erected during his reign (1851–1868) for removing his ceremonial robes and head covering after stepping down from the throne to enter the Audience Room. Before this the golden drapes were hung on the pillars of this small building, which is the same height of the royal baldachin. There is another Arporn Phimok Prasad in Thailand: Rama V had the building copied at his Summer residence, Bang-Pa-In, 60 km north of Bangkok.

Artistically cut miniature trees, mainly around the small park in front of Chakri Maha Prasad, Chinese stone figures and marble terraces are spread throughout the palace grounds.

Past Chakri Maha Prasad once more in an easterly direction one comes upon a few wooden posts painted red and gold. These were hitching posts for the royal elephants. From here the third largest of the accessible buildings is reached. **The Amarin Vinichai Hall.** The complete southern section was reserved for the harem and only the king could enter: even today this part is closed to tourists. This, apparently modest building, at least from the outside, dates back to the first period of building under Rama I, and served originally as the High Court. After the death of this king its function changed and the pompus coronation ceremonies were held in Amarin Vinichai; this still applies today. The hall is also used when the king bestows honours. The complete hall is decorated in turquoise, above the old, golden, Busabok-Mala-Throne, there is a nine-tiered umbrella and a baldachin in the shape of a Mondhop. Today this throne, which is a copy of a chinese junk, is used as an altar. Formerly it was veiled in valuable drapes, when audiences were granted, ceremonial music was heard and after a fanfare the drapes parted and the king appeared in his robes of state, woven with gold threads, like a god before the gathering.

A low wall surrounds the **Maha Montien section.** Just behind Amarin Vinichai, there are two buildings here which were once used for Brahmin cleansing rites. Whilst in the first pavilion holy water was prepared by monks for the king, the second rear pavilion (Pra Tinang Raj Rudee) was of special significance during the crowning ceremonies; it was here, in this small gilded pavilion, with the marble floor, that the head of the monarch was anointed with holy water.

From Maha Montien one comes to a gate which leads to Wat Phra Keo and from here one can see **Borom Pimarn Palace** behind an iron fence. This building, more European in appearance, is today a residence for state guests, and was erected by Rama IX. Ananda Mahidol (1935–1946).

Thailand's first university, the **Wat Po,** borders onto the south of the Grand Palace and be reached from there on foot in a few minutes. This "Temple of the Reclining Buddha" is the largest temple layout in Bangkok, and covers some 8 hectares. Some 300 monks live here The property is divided by the Jetupon Street in two halves, in the one is the accomodation for the monks, and in the other the religious buildings of the monastery. Jetupon Street has an interesting history; it was here that on 6th April 1782, that King Rama I, on the foundation day of the Chakri Dynasty, marched when returning from Cambodia to Thonburi.

The first of these temples, in almost confusing profusion, was in all probability built in the 16th century, it was however Rama I who, in 1793, ordered that building start on the present facilities on the site of the old monastery, and it is said that 12 years were required for completion of these distinctive temples to enhance the new capital, later additions were made under his grandson Rama III.

There are 16 gates in the outside walls of Wat Po, which is also called locally Wat Phra Jetupon; only two of these are open for visitors. Then one is confronted with a confusion of halls and small rooms, prayer rooms and walks, massage school and towers, of which there are an astonishing 95. Viewing Wat Po is fairly simple. Then you don't let yourself be diverted by the various stalls selling all kinds of Thai nick-nacks.

The four largest towers of the 95, those of the **Chedi** are particularly prominent, and are intended to remind the faithful of the building ambitions of the first four Chakri rulers. The Chedi decorated with green mosaic was erected on the orders of Rama I, the loveliest, the blue, dates from the reign of Rama IV, while Rama II had one yellow and one white tower built for himself and his father Rama II. The 71 smaller Chedis of Wat Po house the ashes of various members of the Royal House, and the other 20, important Buddhistic relics.

The greatest sight at Wat Po however is 46 metres (151 ft) long and 15 metres (49 ft) high, built of brick, plastered over with cement and completely covered in gold leaf; the **"Reclining Buddha"**, the colossal figure of the Enlightened One gliding into Nirvana. A gate, guarded by Chinese stone figures, leads to the temple where the effigy can be seen; past the many stalls to the temple entrance, where shoes have to be removed; of special interest on this giant figure, are the soles of his feet which point towards the West.

Inlaid mother-of-pearl, grouped around the Buddhist "Wheel of Knowledge" show the 108 universal symbols of this religion. But not only the giant statue is worth seeing, the wall paintings, poorly preserved, are also interesting. These show scenes of daily life in Thailand of the past and number among the best of traditional Thai paintings.

There ist another custom with a long tradition which is still practiced by childless women at Wat Po today. They address their pleas for children to a black **Lingam** in the courtyard before the entrance to the hall of the "Reclining Buddha". Floral tributes and holy prayer flags signalize that the Lingam as a symbol of fruitfulness – and a symbol of the Hindu god Shiva – is still significant. A hut with an apothecary and the building of the former School of Anatomy flank the Lingam – almost certainly in unintentional symbolism.

From the Lingam, the way then goes to a group of buildings opposite the hall of the "Reclining Buddha". This **Bot** is a hall for religious ceremonies carried out by the monks, and is surrounded by a fence with eight small gates guarded by bronze lions. The outside walls of the main building, which features a red-gold tiered roof, are of special interest. The marble reliefs, from Autthaya, at the base relate episodes from the Ramakien, the Thai version of the Indian Ramayana. Coloured rubbings of these on rice paper can be bought quite cheaply at almost every stall at Wat Po.

Solid teak doors, inlaid with mother-of-pearl lead to the inner of the Bot. And inside frescoes show scenes from the life of Buddha, the ceiling gleams in red and gold, the supporting pillars, which divide the hall with one main and two side aisles are decorated with Siamese motifs. A golden Buddha is enthroned on the altar decorated with gold and green glass. Under this there are said to be the bones of King Rama I as relics.

In the galleries which surround the courtyard of this building there are 394 statues of Buddha, some of them found during excavations at various sites. These galleries also contain the Viharas in which Buddhas of the Ayutthaya and Sukhothai periods are housed.

And throughout the temple area, at almost every turn, holy Bodhi trees of the family Ficus religiosa, vases, shrines and Chinese guard figures dating from the time when Bangkok still had a large Chinese community; many of these small statues however came from China to Thailand as ballast on the rice ships.

Only a few minutes from the Palace, Wat Phra Keo and Wat Po, at Phramane Square, the heart of old Bangkok, a number of major buildings. Past the **University of Fine Arts** (Silapakorn), with a small archaelogical museum and frequent art exhibitions, one reaches the **National Library,** which was housed in the present building (built in 1905) in 1917. The structure originally served as a tribune for spectators at events on Phramane Square, and accommodates today an extensive collection of ancient manuscripts. Most interesting are the palm leaf scrolls topped with artistically carved wood covers.

On the same site there is also **Wat Mahathat** (Temple of the Great Religion), a place of worship which already existed before Bangkok became the capital. After 1782 the brother of Rama I had the building erected in its present form on the site of the ancient temple. Prior to Rama IV's ascent to the throne he spent a large part of his service as a monk here. Today Wat Mahathat is one of the most important Buddhist institutes in the field of meditation.

Between this Wat and the National Museum, **Thammasat University** was founded in 1934 and is considered today leading in the faculties of law, political sciences and economics.

The **National Museum** is one of the biggest and most interesting of Southeast Asia. Its collection of cultural Treasures can be seen daily from 9 a. m. to 12 noon and from 1 p. m. to 4 p. m., Saturdays and Sundays are free of charge.

The museum comprises several old and new buildings, whereby the older of these have an interesting past.

In 1782 the oldest building was erected as the "Palace of the Second King". The Sivamokkha Biman Hall, first on the left of the entrance, served originally as a Hall of Audience, and today accommodates the prehistoric exhibits. Next to the entrance is also the Buddhaisawan Chapel, which the "second King" had erected as a place for meditation. The chapel walls are decorated with paintings depicting scenes from the life of Buddha and the room also houses the bronze statue of Pra Buddha Sihing in Sukhothai style which is greatly revered by the Thais. This system of the "Second King", which was that of a kind of deputy king, was abolished by Rama V. On the other side is the artistic pavilion of King Vajrevudh.

Another important building of the complex is the "Red House" (Tamnak Daeng) which is located behind and slightly to the left of the King's Temple. This was originally in the grounds of the Grand Palace and was the home of Rama I's elder sister. The wooden house was dismantled and rebuilt three times in all, each time at a different place until it finally came to rest at the museum. Inside furnishings give some impression of the life style of the former ruling classes.

Earlier the complete contents of the museum could be accommodated in

The National Museum in Brief:

(New Section)

Hall 22: This houses the splendid funeral coach and litters. The largest funeral coach is 12 metres high and weighs 20 tons. The remarkable about these is that all of them, bearing the urns containing the Kings' ashes, were drawn by men.

Halls 27–35: Objects dating from early Thai kingdoms and art pieces from all parts of Asia. In Halls 32 and 33 special note should be made of the Dvaravati figures of terracotta. Hall 35 contains the Sri Vijaya art influenced by Java. Halls 29 and 31 have stone and bronze figures from Lopburi in Khmer style on show.

Halls 36–41: Objects from Dvaravati and Chiang Saen.

Halls 42–43: Figures from the Sukhothai Period.

Halls 44–45: collection of objects of the Ayutthaya era.

Hall 46: works from the so-called Bangkok (Ratanakosin) Period.

Plus: in Hall 39 coins and bank-notes; in Hall 40 new depictions of Buddha; in Hall 38 textiles; Hall 37 small works of art.

Folders can be obtained at the entrance and there are guided tours in German and English which take around two hours.

---

the beautifully proportioned palace of the "Second King", next to the temple, but today only ethnographic objects are kept here which include furniture, weapons, elephant saddles, porcelain and similar items. A collection of Buddhistic art comprises pieces from several Asian countries.

After leaving the National Museum, a turn to the left and the **National Theatre** is reached.

On special occasions displays of classic forms of Thai Dance Dramas (khon) take place here. A fire destroyed Silpakorn Theatre in 1960, and rebuilding took place 5 years later. If there is the opportunity to see a show at the theatre (season from October to March, mainly at week-ends) then the chance should also be seized to visit the **Nattasin School of Dance** next door. Or perhaps you will be satisfied with a programme of classical drama, which by the way is a far cry from the real thing,

watered down as it were to suit tourists' tastes, at one of the **theatre restaurants** among others the "Piman", "Baan Thai" or "Suwanahong", whilst enjoying a Thai meal.

Close to the Ministry of Defence, almost exactly opposite Wat Phra Keo, there is a small shrine which plays a major role in the lives of Bangkok's citizens; this **Lakmuang** houses the stone column of the same name erected by Rama I as the foundation stone of the new capital. It can also be assumed that this marks the heart of historic Bangkok and all distances in the new city were at one time measured from this spot.

Gamblers are the foremost visitors to Lakmuang Shrine today; driving force being the powers the stone is said to possess to grant wishes (lottery wins). Music and Thai dances are said to win the favour of the stone's spirit, and it goes almost without saying, flowers and joss sticks too. Activities worth watching here reach their climax in the afternoon and early evening.

There are several interesting sights on, or in the immediate vicinity of, Rajdamnoen Avenue, a wide mall almost 4 km (2.5 miles) long, and pride of Bangkok, that leads from Phramane Square to Parliament. Even if not particularly noteworthy the **Monument of Democracy** here simply can't be overlooked. Four mighty pillars range over a chest which – symbolically – holds the Constitution. The monument was erected after the coup of 1932 which introduced democracy to Siam, and sealed the fate of absolute monarchy.

Not far from the monument is **Wat Bovornives** where one of the most historically important Buddha statues, the Jinasri Buddha, is kept.

The "Victorious Buddha" was cast in 1257 when the young Thai kingdom of Sukhothai finally shook off the tyranny of the Cambodian Khmer. Rama II had the statue brought from Phitsanlok to Bangkok when the temple was completed in 1840. King Mongkut, his brother and successor, lived here as abbot for 14 years and founded his Buddhistic Reform Movement which still exists here.

Worthy of a closer look are the main gates, decorated with bearded Chinese demons; one was gilded later by Chinese opium merchants to win the gods' favours for opium trading.

Wat Rachanada is interesting for its **amulette** market (close to the Golden Mount in Mahchai Street). Most natives of Thailand wear an amulette of some kind or other, not always motivated by Buddhism, and they are chosen with great care since they are believed to have powers of protection; they are for the most part tiny terracotta figures of Buddha sealed in plastic. Certain amulettes said to possess

special powers are extremely expensive for Thai pockets and cost thousands of Baht. Rama III had Wat Rachanada built for his niece Princess Somanat Vattana Wadi.

The major attraction at the cloister **Wat Indram** close to the junction of Rajdamneon and Krang Kasen Road, is the 33 metre (108'3") high statue of Buddha created in 1830 of brick, plastered over and painted yellow. From a tower at the rear of the giant figure – close to the head – there is a marvellous view over the roofs of Bangkok.

Wat Benchamabopitr, also called Marble Temple, is possibly the most gracious of all the capital's religious buildings and it is at the same time the newest of all royal temples. Building was started in 1901 during the reign of Chulalongkorn, but was only completed 10 years after his death. It is the seat of the Patriarch of Siam, head of religious hierarchy.

Although the structure of classic Thai architecture is not evident throughout, European influences are harmonious; the courtyard paved in marble and the ever present doves bring a breath of Italy. Two marble lions (Rajasingha, Burmese: Cinthe) in traditional Burmese style guard the entrance to the Bot under a projecting tiered roof, which in this instance is also supported by pillars. These pillars plus floors and steps are of white Carrara marble which Chulalongkorn had shipped from Italy.

Dominating the inner room is a golden Buddha, a copy of the famous Buddha Jinaraj. Under the altar at its base, an urn containing a portion of King Chulalongkorn's ashes was buried. A very special atmosphere is created inside by the murals and frescos.

Probably the most impressive aspect however are the cloisters with a respectable collection of 51 Buddha figures, some genuine, others copies, representing not only Thailand but also other Buddhistic countries. Especially famous is that of the fasting Buddha, the so-called "Hunger Buddha".

A giant Bodhi tree spreads its holy branches behind the courtyard and legend has it that this tree came from shoots brought from Ceylon in 1871 and it is an offshoot of that very tree in the North of India where enlightenment came to Buddha.

A canal, where water turtles swim, separates the religious section of Wat Benchamabopitr from the monks' cells. King Rama IX, the reigning monarch, served as a monk here only a short time after his coronation. A tip for photographers: really good pictures can be taken from the bridge over this canal.

At a square at the north end of Rajdamnoen Avenue is an **equestrian statue** of Rama V which was cast in France and erected here during his lifetime (Rama V = King Chulalongkorn). From here one can see the dome of the former throne room which has served as the seat of Thailand's **parliament** since 1933. The building was designed by an Italian architect in Renaissance style and completed in 1916 during the reign of Rama VI.

Dusit Zoo, well known for its chimpanzee show, was installed on an artificial mound north-east of the parliament building and is popular among the Thais particularly on Sundays. This is where the royal white elephants were, and still are, kept in a special compound and on a specially selected diet; in bygone days the power of the king was also measured by the number of white elephants he owned. Although in fact white is the wrong description for these beasts, they are really pinkish albinos with red eyes.

At the centre of parklike grounds with an artificial lake, east of Rama V

Road, there rises **Chitralada Palace,** the Royal Residence. This is not open to the public and the traditional character of the building can only be guessed at from outside. An odd fact; the grounds also house an experimental farm for dairy cows.

Only very few tourists visit **Wat Rajabopitr,** in spite of the fact that it represents an architectural exception. It is located close to the Ministry of the Interior on Khlong Lawd. Innumerable pigeons are fed here by the faithful for the benefit of their souls. Landmark of the Wat is the high, central Chedi which is reminiscent of Nakhon Pathom which includes the oldest Buddhist sanctuary of the country.

Wat Rajabopitr had already been erected before King Chulalongkorn's first visit to Europe, but for all that displays evidence of the efforts of just this king to integrate western styles into Thai structures. Thus this Wat with its annexes can be seen as the forerunner of Wat Benchamabopitr which was built 40 years later. The temple was also chosen by King Prajadhipok for meditation and his ashes are buried here.

Not far away there is a square where two large red, richly decorated wood masts, joined by an equally richly decorated beam, stand, This square of the **Great Swing** (Sao Ching Cha) was until before World War II (1932) the scene of a ceremony based on Hinduism which was later forbidden no doubt because of the danger involved. Two teams of four men competed in swinging so high on the ropes until they were not only in a horizontal position but were also able to reach for a bag of money fixed to a bamboo pole 20 metres above the ground.

Opposite the Great Swing is **Wat Suthat,** in which three kings influenced building. The sanctuary was started in 1782 under Rama I and only completed under Rama III. It is famed for its Bot 80 metres (262 ft.) long on a double terrace. Inside in addition to a large golden Buddha there are lifesize effigies of 80 of his followers. Doors and windows are decorated with Hindu scenes but the wall paintings show scenes from Buddha's life. The Wat is closed except on Buddhist holidays.

Also of interest is the great Viharn which is surrounded by a gallery of gilded Buddha statues. The main figure is that of Buddha Shakayamuni cast in the 14th century in Sukhothai and brought to Bangkok by Rama I. Wooden doors, almost 6 metres (19'8") high, close the Viharn, the carving is said to have been carried out by Rama II, who, legend has it, ordered that the tools be destroyed to prevent copies being made. The terrace of the Virharn is decorated with Chinese figures brought as ballast on the rice junks from the North.

A climb up to the **Golden Mount,** an artificial rise close to Wat Suthat, is rewarding. For quite some time this was the highest point, 78 metres (256 ft), in the capital and it can only be reached over 318 steps. Rama III decided to have the mound made in Bangkok in the same way as the Peking Coal Mounds in the north of the emperor's city. A golden Chedi at the top houses relics of Buddha which Rama V received from the former Viceroy of India.

It's also worth climbing up to the Chedi even if the building itself is closed. There is an unhindered view of all Bangkok and the monastery **Wat Sraket** which was built under Rama I. This Wat on the east slope of the mound was originally erected during the Ayutthaya Period, and it is said that Rama I stopped here on the way to his coronation at Thonburi for a ritual cleansing ceremony. Special note should be made of the beautifully carved teak doors of the Viharn.

Anyone wanting to buy gold should visit the **Chinese quarter.** Bordered by the roads Charoen Krung (New Road) and Yaowaraj, there are innumerable shops in this large area offering gold, and above all jewellry, at fairly reasonable prices. Thailand's four million Chinese are considered the largest of all ethnic minorities and have had great financial success mainly with small businesses.

Gold also dominates in the main Chinese temple of the quarter. In **Wat Trimitr** a Buddha of the Sukhothai era weighing 5,500 kilos (12.125 lbs) and to 80% pure gold, has been erected, which by the way was found by chance. During work on Bangkok's harbour the 3 metre (9'10") high statue was uncovered and at the time no one was aware of the real value because a thick layer of plaster covered the gold. In this way it was transported without any real interest to Wat Trimitr, but on arrival there was a cloudburst and the plaster softened. When transportation was resumed the figure fell and crashed to the ground, the plaster crumbled and the gold shone through. It is assumed that the figure was plastered over in the 18th century to conceal its real value from Burmese intruders. But, even the Thais let themselves be misled for 200 years.

Misleading too, at least occasionally, are the activities at the **Thieves Market,** which is actually called Nakorn Kasem and also in the Chinese quarter. The name is however confusing; stolen goods are almost certainly not offered here, on the other hand the pull of the antique shops on tourists, is that much greater. They swarm here fascinated by the treasures on show and quite often let themselves be blinded. The rule is bargaining.

Not every tourist will think that **Jim Thompson's Thai House** on Khlong Maha Nag and the end of Soi Kasemsong II, numbers among the great sights of Bangkok. Nevertheless this collection of seven houses built in Thai style by the well known American, do count among the capital's attractions. Jim Thompson came to Thailand after the end of World War II and built up the country's silk industry. In 1967 during a visit to Malaysia he disappeared under mysterious circumstances which haven't been explained until the present day.

The houses and the remarkable art collection of Thompson can be viewed in the morning. Admission charges are for the benefit of a School for the Blind. A short stroll through the gardens is also worthwhile and one gets the impression of a miniature tropical paradise.

Flower lovers can feast their eyes at other places too. First and foremost at **Thevet Flower Market,** where the plant life of Thailand, which flourishes so well, can be admired in full. Stands offer flowers and plants and with certainty some of the 1,000 species of Thai orchids are also offered.

Much less flowery on the other hand, and that for some years now, are the famous Bangkok **Khlongs,** and its twin on the other side of the river, Thonburi. Many of the canals which were so typical of the city have had to make way for roads, so that the name "The Venice of Asia", applies less and less.

But don't be put off, a Khlong trip – even when seasoned Bangkok travellers advise against it – should be on every tourist's programme. Certainly the exotic "floating markets" have degenerated into subjects for tourists' cameras and life on the remaining Khlongs is

less lively and colourful; and is becoming less and less so.

One of the most interesting Khlongs in Bangkok itself is **Khlong Saen Sap,** which was built by the first ruler to open a way to the sea and thus Cambodia. One of the small narrow boats (Long tails = hang yao) can best be rented at the Ekamai Bridge (at Soi 63 on Sikhumvit Road) or Prakanong Khlong Tan Bridge (Soi 71 of the same road). Especially recommended is a trip in a southerly direction to the rural areas; here there are still typical Thai houses on the banks and one can catch a glimpse of Thai family life.

The best and most rewarding water trips are however offered at **Thonburi** and often include a visit to the "floating markets" – above all in the early morning – combined with a view of the royal barges and Wat Arun. Trips start at the landing stage behind the "Oriental Hotel" or at the river station near Phramane Square. Bookings can be made at most of the better hotels or a travel agency.

First the high spirited trip takes off down the Menam in a welter of waves and then along the Khlong Thao Khanong. After about one hour the floating markets are reached, at one time a considerable financial factor and now only a tourist attraction. The return trip is for the most part via Khlong Dan and Khlong Bangkok Yai to the Menam ending a short way upriver at **Wat Arun.** This "Temple of the Evening Twilight" with 79 metre (259'2") high tower (Prang) became a landmark of Bangkok, and in fact is in Thonburi. Wat Cheng, the former name, was already a Chinese temple before Thonburi became the capital after the destruction of Ayutthaya by the Burmese. After restoration for the first time in 1780, Rama II reached a decision to

161

have Wat Arun built as it stands today, and building was finally completed under Rama III.

The 79 metre (259'2") high centre tower, which was erected on one originally only 15 metres (49 ft) high, is completely covered in coloured shards of Chinese porcelain. Together with glass tiles and plaster work they form flowers and garlands, ghosts and fabulous creatures. The tower can be reached via four steep stairways and from around 50 metres (164 ft.) there's a marvellous view of the temples and river.

Around the middle tower are four smaller Prangs of a similar shape, four pavilions in the lower third of the main tower are decorated with scenes from the life of the historic founder of Buddhism (Shakayamuni Buddha): birth, enlightenment, sermons and death (entrance into Nirvana). Niches in the upper section house depictions of the Hindu god Indra on the three-headed elephant Erewan and the moon god Soma.

Inside are several good wall paintings and grim Yaks (guard figures) watch over the entrance to the Viharn, formerly the scene of impressive ceremonies; at the end of the rainy season the King, within the Festival of Tot Kathin, arrived on a ceremonial barge at Wat Arun bringing robes and other gifts for the monks.

The **Royal Barges** are usually visited after visiting Wat Arun. The largest of these, Sri Supannahong, is 45 metres (148 ft.) long with a mythological swan as a figurehead; a crew of 54 oarsmen, 2 helmsmen, 2 officers, a flag officer and a singer, were needed to bring the King on his throne to Wat Arun, with his gifts for the monks. Today the barges are kept in a boathouse, the valuable carvings are sorely in need of restoration and they can't always be seen in passing.

For some years now trips have been offered to the "floating markets" of **Damnoen Saduak,** about one hour from Bangkok in a south-westerly direction in the province of Ratchaburi, where activities on the water are somewhat lively. These trips are usually combined with a visit to the Chedi at **Nakhon Pathom** and sometimes also with a trip to the Bridge on the **River Kwai** near Kanchanaburi; the bamboo bridge built by prisoners of war with great loss of life no longer exists, having made way for an iron bridge some 100 metres (328 ft) further upriver, which was built while the country was still under Japanese occupation and after partial destruction during bombardment in 1945, rebuilt by the Thais. Some 7,000 war dead have found their last resting place at two well cared for military cemeteries at Kanchanaburi, for the most part victims of the Kwai Bridge and the "Death Railway". This railway was to be led over the Three Pagoda Pass to Burma to ensure supplies to Japanese troops there.

Another interesting trip is offered by the hotel "Oriental" on the hotel-owned **"Oriental Queen"** which travels the Menam to Ayutthaya. Part of the trip is by ship and the reminder by bus. Another worthwhile trip is that by bus in the morning via Bang-Pa-In (Royal Summer Residence) to Ayutthaya and return, with lunch included on the "Oriental Queen" to Bangkok, at the landing stage behind the hotel. Just a word of warning: the air conditioning on the boat has cooled many a tourist's enthusiasm for Thailand with a hefty cold. Bangkok is reached around 5 p.m.

Every Wednesday the "Queen" sets off on a "candlelight cruise", with a trip starting on the Menam at 8 p.m. which takes about three hours. During dinner-dancing a pleasant impression of Bangkok and Thonburi by night.

Hardly candlelit on the other hand is Bangkok's **night life,** on the contrary gaudy glaring neon is more likely. In the famous-notorious streets of Patpong I and Patpong II near Silom Road, and in the new quarter springing up around the Soi Cowboy, it really is gaudy; one bar after another, barkers (do yourself a favour and don't fall for their quick spiel) offer the for the greater part, unaccompanied man, all that which is otherwise banned in puritanical Thailand. In all the bars there are girls from all parts of the country dancing to the latest hits and there for one thing, or maybe two, only, to turn night into day and make life pleasant, for cash, for the foreigner. The bars change hands frequently, many are owned by foreigners, and the quality of the individual establishments varies strongly. Several discreet hotels in the direct vicinity of both Patpong roads offer stays by the hour, which for additional charge can be spread throughout the night. If the girls leave the bars before official closing time (for the most part 1 a.m.) then that has its price too. Girl and hotel of course cost extra for their services. Amidst all the excitement of what's offered so freely it doesn't hurt to remember that the girls have landed in the oldest profession out of sheer financial necessity and they deserve to be treated with gentlemanly courtesy. Drunken, loud, or in any other way offensive, foreigners are regarded with distaste.

Two of the best massage salons in Bangkok are on Patpong II.

The first of these facilities was founded around 20 years ago and today Bangkok is considered the "massage Babel" of the world. Hundreds of them offer their services to the, mostly not at all, physically exhausted; and lately several have expanded to include female clients.

Quality of the individual salons ranges from disgustingly dirty to palaces of marble and glass, and the skill of the masseuse varies just as much. What should be remembered is that in principal these are not prostitutes. Although, the girls in white overalls with a number on the lapel, shut in so-called "Fishtanks" behind one-way glass windows, they can only be seen through from outside, are as a rule ready to perform other "services". Genuine massage takes on average about one hour.

Part of Bangkok's amusement quarter by night are also the ladies who turn out to be exactly the opposite at second glance. These attractive male-ladies stroll provocatively along the Silom and approach male tourists. They are called "kra toes" in Thailand (transvestites) and many a one has regretted his adventure with them at the latest in the early hours of the morning when he finds his plundered wallet.

Dancing fans are best served at the discos of the big hotels, even when it's a little more expensive it's worthwhile just to see the show put on by Thai, and often Filipino, combos.

A pleasure of another kind and another side of Bangkok's nightlife is offered by the restaurants. There are any number of these along the main shopping streets and close to the international hotels. From Austrian to Chinese, Swiss to Burmese, the range is almost bewildering and the question that comes up at mealtimes in Bangkok is not where, but much more often what.

A reliable answer is found in the what's-on booklets.

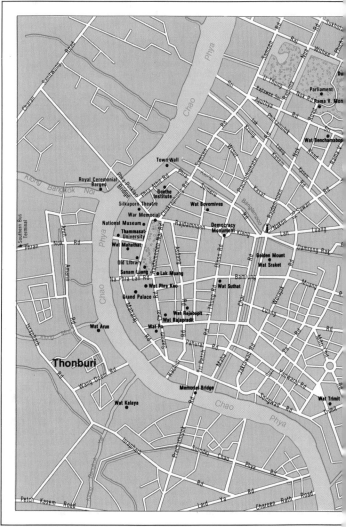

BANGKOK (KRUNG THEP)

0   0,5 km

0   0,5 miles

Northern Bus Terminal

Airport

Highway

Nakhon Chaisri Road

Rama VI Rd

Sukhotai Rd

Soi 2

Soi 5

Ari Soi 2

Ari Soi

Inthalup Yothin Road

Chitralada Palace

Withee Road

Yothi Road

Dindeeng Rd

Rajanam

Rama VI Rd

Rai Rd

Sawaatkhalok Rd

Sri Ayuthya Rd

Sri Ayuthya Rd

Suan-Pakkard-Palace

Petchburi

Matasan

Road

Eastern Bus Terminal

Phya Nak Rd

Rama VI Rd

Soi Charoem

Road

(New) Petchburi Road

Jim Thompson's Thai House

Phya Thai Rd

Road

Rama I Road

Rama I Road

Erawan-Hotel

Soi 4

Soi 1

Sri Chula 2

Soi Chula 12

Pihenchit Road

Karnen

Sri Chula 3

Rama VI

Muang Rd

Thai Rd

Chulalongkorn University

Dunant Rd

Raj Damri

Langsuan

Soi Ruamrudi

Ruamrudi

Road

Rama VI

Sri Chula 13

Snake Farm

Sri Chula 14

Rama IV Road

Henri

Raj Damri Rd

Sarasin Soi

Wireless

Polo Soi

Phya Road

Surawong Road

Silom Road

Rama IV Road

Lumpini-Park

Chidlom Rd

Pattaya

165

Thailand, Burma –
from A to Z

The letter and number following each place name is a cross reference to the folded map.
* = see map on reverse

Akyab (*E1) also called Sittwe. Capital of Arakan with strong Moslem influence (Pop. 40,000). Founded in 1826 by the British General Morrison at the month of the River Kaladan. No places of special interest.

Amarapura (*D3) also called Taungmyo; as the "City of Immortals" under King Bodawpaya (1782-1819) for the first time capital of the Konbaung Dynasty; around 10 km (6 mi.) from Mandalay, Amarapura was once more capital under the kings Tharawaddy and Pagan Min between 1837 and 1878. Only very little remains of the palaces, and a few small pagodas can be seen. After a walk over the teak built U Pein Bridge (1,200 m / 3,936 ft.) one reaches the Kyauktawgyi Pagoda close to the village of Taung De; the pagoda built in 1847 houses a fine alabaster Buddha and wall paintings, which also depict the arrival of the Portuguese in Burma; the pagoda was built exclusively by Birmans based on the Ananda Temple at Pagan. Also in Amarapura a Chinese temple (Joss House), the Nagayon Pagoda with a dragon's head crowning the stupa, the Pahtodawgyi Pagoda and the village of Kyi Thun Khat famed for wrought iron work. Amarapura, also well known for weaving, has some 10,000 inhabitants.

Amherst (*H4) beach resort 45 km (28 miles) south of Moulmein, the beach at Setse was particularly popular with the Britisch colonialists; a new beach hotel is said to be planned, 20 km (12.5 miles) south, close to the town of Thanvyuzayat. There is a military cemetery where those prisoners of war are buried who died during building of the River Kwai railway.

Ao Luk (*H2) on the South-west coast of Thailand is the starting point for a trip through Than Bokkoroni National Park, considered one of the most beautiful in the country; the bay of Ao Luk is also fascinating because of the bizarre chalk cliffs.

Arakan State (E1–H2) between the Arakan Mountains and the Gulf of Bengal. Mount Victoria is the highest 3,053 m (10,016 ft.). Wonderful sandy beaches in the south, above all at Sandoway with beach hotel. Conquered in 1782 by the Konbaung King Bodawpaya, two years later his troops brought the venerated Maha Muni Buddha, in three sections, to Amarapura, where 8 km (5 miles) away the pagoda of the same name was built and connected to the royal palace with a covered walk (main attraction in Mandalay). Capital of Arakan is Akyab.

Ava (*D3) where the Irrawaddy meets with the River Myitnge close to Amarapura; can only be reached by boat during the monsoon season. After the fall of Pagan (1287) a new Birman centre was formed here. Founded in 1364 it was, until the middle of the 17th century, the main city of Upper Burma, then for one hundred and fifty years capital of the second Burmese kingdom (Taungu); main sights: part of the old city walls with the "Gate of the Hair Washing Ceremony" (northern gate); "leaning tower" of Ava; Maha Aungmye Bonzan Monastery, the best preserved building (renovated in 1873); Htilainshin Pagoda erected by the Pagan King Kyanzittha; Leitutgyi Pagoda and Lawatharaphu Pagoda. North of the town, the Ava Bridge, built by the British in 1934 and blown up in 1942 (rebuilt in 1954) crosses the Irrawaddy.

Ayutthaya (D3) 74 km north of Bangkok, interesting remains with temple ruins dating back to the second great Thai dynasty; it is said that at the peak of its powers there were 375 temples, 3 palaces and 29 forts here. A must in every tourist's itinerary. Road, rail and ship connections with Bangkok. Sights: Wat Mahatat, Wat Rachaburana, Phra Mongkol Bophitr (seated bronze Buddha), Wat Phra Ram, Wat Sri Sanphet (three white stupas), Wat Phramane, Chao Sanphya National Museum.

Ban Chiang (B4) village 47 km (29 miles) east of Udon Thani in the north-

east of Thailand. Archaeological finds of pre-historic burial grounds, considered the oldest rural civilisation of the Bronze Age. Bones, pottery, weapons and tools of iron and copper found. Scientists assume that the first use of bronze took place in South-east Asia and not as was previously believed in Mesopotamia. The objects, some 8,000 years old, are on exhibit at a small museum.

Bangkok (E3) capital of Thailand and seat of the Chakri Dynasty since 1782; at present ruled by Rama IX. Population some 5 millions, modern city of a western style with only a few remaining canals (khlong); one tenth of the total population of the country lives here. Mainly impressive for shopping facilities and night-life. The airport Dom Muang is some 20 km (12.4 miles) outside. Numerous luxury and first class hotels and plenty of accommodation

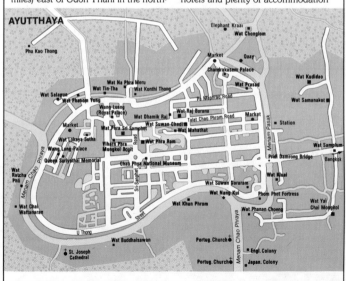

167

for more modest purses. Not typical of Thailand as a city. Sights: Royal Palace (no shorts, shirt sleeves rolled down!). Wat Phra Keo, Wat Arun (at Thonburi), Wat Po, Wat Trimitr, Lak Muang (patron spirit temple), Wat Benchamabopitr (Marble Temple), Dusit Zoo, National Museum (!), Chinese quarter, Jim Thompson's Thai House. Shopping and sightseeing programme in the capital on the Chao Phaya (Menam) with the sister town of Thonburi on the other bank of the river can be done in 3 days. Shows of classic Thai dance at the restaurants "Piman", "Baan Thai" and "Suwanahong".

Bang-Pa-In (D3) summer palace of the Royal Family with 5 main buildings around 60 km (37 miles) north of Bangkok in parklike grounds, not very interesting architecturally.

Bang Saen (E3) beach resort, popular among Thais, on the eastern Gulf of Thailand with 18 hole golf course; motor boats to the island Ko Sichang with former royal Summer Palace and good diving facilities; the Beach Hotel is recommendable without being luxurious.

Bang Saray (E3) Fisher village a few kilometres south of Pattaya with a nice beach for those seeking peace and quiet; possibilities for water sports. Golf course, restaurants and bungalows.

Ban Keo (E2) small town near Kanchanaburi with excavations dating back to the Neolithic Period.

Bassein (*H2) with around 140,000 inhabitants the biggest town on the Irrawaddy Delta; known for exports of rice and jute and manufacture of colourful umbrellas and pottery; 112 km (69.5 miles) from the Gulf of Bengal. Can best be reached by ship from Rangoon (18 hours, twice daily service) or by air. During the 2nd Anglo-Burmese war the British built a fort here: The Shwemakhtaw Pagoda at the town centre is visited by many pilgrims.

Beikthano ruined city, some 140 km (87 miles) from Prome, of the Pyu people, is reputed to be older than Sri Ksetra. King Duttabaung founder of Sri Ksetra is said to have destroyed Beikthano; the town was considered the "City of Vishnu".

Bhamo (*C4) some 50 km (31 miles) from borders of the People's Republic of China; with 10,000 inhabitants is the main trading town for the tribes settled in the area, Shan, Kachin, Lisu, Palaung, plus Indians and Chinese. Bhamo has the reputation of being the centre of smuggling between Burma/China. The Irrawaddy is navigable to here.

Bor Sang (B2) 9 km (5.5 miles) east of Chiang Mai known as a centre for wood carvers and umbrella makers; the best silk and cotton mills are close-by.

Chaiya (H2) small, sleepy, provincial town 640 km (397 miles) from Bangkok. No good accomodation. But the latest research has shown that Chaiya was once the capital of the powerful marine kingdom of Sri Vijaya, which was hitherto assumed as being Palembang on Sumatra. From the 7th to 11th centuries this power ruled most of South-east Asia. Wat Mahatat in Chaiya displays clear signs of Javanese influence and the Chedi is said to be more than 1,300 years old.

Chakangrao (C2) old city in the central plains of Thailand opposite Kamphaeng Phet on the other side of the Ping River. Sights: Wat Chedi Klang Tung.

Chanthaburi (E,F4) known for its sapphire and ruby mines, 330 km (205 miles) from Bangkok on the eastern Gulf; many businesses engaged in polishing precious stones. A few kilometres south, old fortifications erected by Taksin after the fall of Ayutthaya.

Chiang Dao (A2) 72 km (45 miles) north of Chiang Mai with caves of the same name in which effigies of Buddha

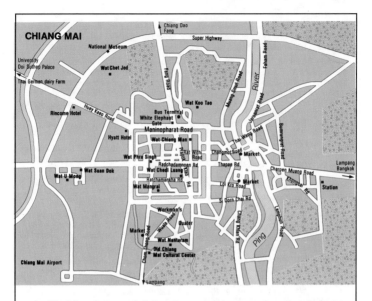

CHIANG MAI

and a Chedi have been erected; there is an elephant school in the vicinity.

Chiang Mai (B2) population around 105,000, second largest town in Thailand, some 780 km (484 miles) north of Bangkok. "Pearl of the North" believed to be Thailand's prettiest town, cooler than the South at the foot of the 1,876 m (6,155 ft.) Doi Suthep with the loveliest temple of North Thailand. Temples, craftsmanship, mountain tribes and wonderful landscapes, are all reasons for a stay of several days. Founded in 1296 by King Mangrai the town on the River Ping, flourished until conquered by the Birmans in 1556, as the capital of the Lan-na realms. Within the city walls, remains of which are still evident, were the royal residence, the palaces of nobles and administration buildings. Sights: temple on Doi Sthep perhaps the most impressive of Thai

sacral structures; from there by jeep to a Meo village and the opportunity to buy examples of their handicrafts; sights to see in the town: Wat Chedi Luang, Wat Phra Singh, Wat Chiang Man, Wat Ku Dao, Wat Suan Dork, Wat Jet Yort, the Museum. First class shopping facilities (at times better than in Bangkok) for silk, lacquer ware, precious stones, antiques. There are hotels of all classes.

Chiang Rai (A2) capital of the northernmost Thai province around 940 km (583 miles) from Bangkok. Of great strategic importance due to closeness to Laos and Burma. The town (Pop. 12,000) was built in 1262 by King Mangrai even before Chiang Mai and lies on the River Kok, which is ideal for boat trips to villages of ethnic minorities. Only two temples are worth visiting: Wat Prasing and Wat Phra Keo.

Chiang Rai has one good, and several acceptable, hotels. Trips by jeep to the mountain tribes (Akha, Yao, Lisu, Meo).

Chiang Saen (A2) located on a loop of the River Mekong, has a great past and little future; already in the 10th century, it is said, the town (today some 1,000 inhabitants) was one of the first permanent settlements of the Thai, the town was fortified in the 13th/14th centuries. In 1238 the Thai ruler Mangrai was born here who turned the county taken over from his father, into a nation. In 1262 he founded from here Chiang Rai; in 1281 he occupied the Mon realms of Haripunchai; fifteen years later he founded Chiang Mai (1296). Later Chiang Saen was conquered by the Burmese. Rama I, founder of the Chakri Dynasty in Bangkok reconquered the town but ordered its destruction. In 1957 Chiang Saen was made county town without any possibility for economic development because of its location right on the border to Laos. Extensive ruins and a small museum are testimonies of a great past. Trips can be arranged from Chiang Rai. Overnight stays at Chiang Saen are not recommended.

Chin State (*D1) on the border to Bangladesh and India, home of the people of the same name (numbering around 350,000). It was the British who first brought the Chin into contact with the outside world because of their skill as soldiers; the people are divided into Northern and Southern Chin and are mainly occupied in the cultivation of rice and maize; the Naga people, notorious headhunters in the past, are also settled in Chin State.

Chon Buri (E3) a lively provincial town on the eastern Gulf of Thailand (Pop. 50,000), with two ancient temples at the town centre (Wat Dhama Nimitr and Wat Intharami); 80 km (50 miles) from Bangkok the road turns off at

Chon Buri for the beach resort Bang Saen (see there). The coast at Chon Buri is a centre of oyster fishing.

Chumphon (G2) small fishing port at the mouth of the river of the same name. Arrangements are made here for boat trips to the cliffs on islands where swallows nests are collected, so highly esteemed in Chinese cuisine. Interesting scenes during the mating season from March to August.

Damnoen Saduak (E2) small village around 100 km (62 miles) from Bangkok. Rewarding trips by boat to the "floating markets", with many varieties of fruits and vegetables, are arranged here.

Diamond Island (*H2) at the mouth of the Bassein River (Ngawun); some 100 km from Bassein where turtles lay thousands of eggs on the beaches.

Fang (A2) town at the edge of the "Golden Triangle" around 150 km (93 miles) from Chiang Mai on the border to Burma; is considered a major support point in opium smuggling and is, with neighbouring Tha Thon – only for the adventurous – starting point for boat trips on the Kok to Chiang Rai; the Yao tribe lives in the mountains around Fang.

Golden Triangle (A2) formed by the borders of Thailand, Laos and Burma; notorious for opium cultivation by the tribes settled there.

Gulf of Martaban (*H3,4) starts at the mouth of the Sittang, extreme borders are the Irrawaddy Delta and the mouth of the Salween.

Gulf of Thailand (F,G2–4) is formed by the Malaysian Peninsula and the eastern Thailand, Cambodian and Vietnam coasts, then becomes part of the South China Seas.

Haad Yai (A7) (Pop. 70,000) 1,300 km (806 miles) south of Bangkok on the

Malayan Peninsula and only 60 km (37 miles) from the Malaysian border is economic centre of southern Thailand. Rubber plantations, tin mines, lots of stores and a lively night life. Worth seeing is the "Rubber Research Centre" showing refining and new methods of tapping rubber. The starting point for trips to the beach at Singkhla, 30 km (19 miles) away; several good hotels and restaurants (sharks' fin soup famous), can be reached from Bangkok by road, rail or air.

Halin (*D3) ancient Pyu ruins around 20 km (12.5 miles) south-east of Shwebo; according to legend destroyed in a rain of ash. Similar to the other two historic places Sri Ksetra and Beikthano; scientific estimates are that Halin dates back to between 200 and 600 A.D.

Heho (*E4) airport in the Shan State with a small town; starting point for trips to Taunggyi, Kalaw and Inle Lake, flights take place from Mandalay and Rangoon.

Hot (B1) around 90 km (56 miles) south-west of Chiang Mai; a town of wooden huts, the old town was located 15 km (9 miles) away at the junction of the Ping and Chedi rivers and was a reminder of the town's past as part of the northern Thai realms.

Hua Hin (F2) popular beach resort around 230 km (143 miles) from Bangkok, frequented above all by the Thais themselves; the royal summer palace is close to the fine white beach; well known sailing regattas take place from here, many types of sports, good accommodation in picturesque fishing villages.

Huay Yang (F2) waterfalls close to Prachuab Khiri Khan at the narrowest point in Thailand (13 km/8 miles); also the cliffs of Khao Chong Krachok are close by; boat trips and cliff climbing at sunrise; bungalows available.

Inle Lake (*E4) in the Shan State, see special chapter for description.

Kachin State (*A,B4) in extreme North of the country home of many ethnic minorities, the Jingphaw (actually Kachin), Shan, Lashi, Kadu, Kanang, Tailay; they are animists and nomadic farmers.

Kalaw (*E3) once a popular "hill station" among the British, today a sleepy provincial town around 35 km (22 miles) from the airport at Heho; excursions to the Palaung villages and the Buddhist cult caves at Pindaya (numerous ancient statues of Buddha) start here.

Kamphaeng Phet (C2) town on the River Ping which was in the past the major outpost of the kingdom of Sukhothai; there are ruins dating back to this time: major sights of interest: Wat Phra Keo and Wat Phrathat. Good overnight accomodation.

Kanchanaburi (E2) 130 km (81 miles) west of Bangkok (Pop. 15,000). The name comes from the ore mines on the vicinity which made the town rich; lies where the small and the great Kwae Rivers meet, which from here becomes the Maeklong. The small Kwae became known worldwide as the River Kwai; there are two well cared for cemetries in the town with the graves of 7,000 prisoners of war who died building the railroad; the famous Bridge on the River Kwai is in the west of the town.

Karen State (*G,H4) around one third of the Burmese Karen live here, close to the border with Thailand.

Kayah State (*F4) main food markets of the Red Karen (75,000) the former princedoms, which were administered under a British protectorate, were combined to form Kayah State in 1951; the Kayah enjoy today similar minority rights as the Shan.

Khao Yai (D3,4) National Park, an extensive wooded area some 2,200 square kilometres (850 square miles) around the 1,330 m (4,364 ft.) high Khao Laem; pathways to various waterfalls, rest houses and bungalows.

Klaeng: birthplace of a famous Thai poet; has a huge new temple with a colourful roof.

Ko Chang (F4) an island lying off the province of Trang bordering onto Kampuchea (Cambodia); around 400 km (248 miles) from Bangkok with fine coral reefs.

Ko Mak (F4) see under Koh Chang.

Ko Kut (F4) see under Koh Chang.

Ko Si Chang (E3) island off Si Rache on the East Coast of Thailand, with good deep sea diving.

Ko Phuket (A6) at the south-westerly tip of Thailand connected to the mainland by a bridge; 30,000 inhabitants, can be reached from Bangkok in 14 hours by bus. An increasingly popular holiday resort with several first class beaches, good accommodation and plenty of opportunitites for sport; the town of Phukhet is picturesquely built in Sino-Portuguese style.

Ko Samui (G,H2) large island in the Gulf of Thailand there are daily ferries from Surat Thani to Ang Thong on the island; white sandy beaches, coconut palm jungles, fishing villages; simple accommodation. Interesting for tourists.

Kubua (E2) some 10 km (6 miles) from the town of Rat Buri; important historic finds; temple of the Dvaravati Period excavated.

Kyaikto (*G4) small town between Pegu and Thaton, starting point for excursions to the "Golden Cliffs" of Kyaik-tiyo, which are reached after a march lasting six hours; 5.5 m (18 ft.) high stupa was erected on a gilded rock at the edge of a cliff. Accommodation only at the monastery hostel.

Kyaukme (*D4) town in northern Burma where the great Shan festival

takes place each year in March.

Lampang (B2) Pop. 50,000, city around 100 km (62 miles) from Chiang Mai; structures show evidence of extended Burmese occupation. Historic town centre with lovely temples, typical horse drawn coaches. Good overnight accommodation.

Lamphun (B2) 26 km (16 miles) south of Chiang Mai with one of the loveliest temples of the North: Wat Haripunchai. The town has a population of around 12,000 today and was from the 8th century until conquered by Mang Rai in 1281, capital of the Mon realms of Haripunchai; according to stories handed down was laid out in the form of a sea shell in the 6th century by the monk Suthepa Reussi; the prettiest girls in Thailand are said to come from here and the neighbouring towns.

Lashio (*C4) in the north of Burma, from here the road built during World War II leads to Yunnan "Burma Road"; the market is the meeting place of the northern Shan tribes.

Lop Buri (D3) major town some 150 km (93 miles) north of Bangkok; between the 6th and 11th centuries main town of Mon-Dvaravati and a great city under the Khmer kings as capital of the Thai provinces; further highpoint under King Narai (1656–1688/Ayutthaya Dynasty) who feared an attack on Ayutthaya by the Europeans from the sea, and made Lop Buri second seat of government; Narai's Greek minister Constantine Phaulkon had palaces and fortifications built. Places of interest: Prang Sam Yod (Temple of the Three Towers), Wat Sri Ratana Mahatat (monastery), Hindu Temple, Palace complex with museum. Not very good accommodation.

Mae Sai (A2) northernmost town in Thailand, together with Ciang Saen the peak of the "Golden Triangle"; Burmese come over the border to shop, and goods from Laos and Burma are smuggled in.

Mae Sariang (B1) around 200 km (124 miles) south-west of Chiang Mai a town which still has a great deal of originality. From here hikes into the mountain regions to the nomadic mountain tribes.

Mae Sot (C1) only 5 km (3 miles) from the Burmese border with richly decorated temples in Burmese style in the vicinity. Busy trading centre for Burmese and Thais alike.

Mandalay (*D3) with a population of around 50,000 the second largest city in Burma and some 620 km (384 miles) north of Rangoon. Centre point of Burmese Buddhism; lies on the Irrawaddy with interesting teak wharves; is considered the most interesting Burmese city. The history of Mandalay is short but full; founded in 1857 by King Mindon and from 1860 to 1885 capital of the Konbaung Dynasty, the last king, Thibaw went into Indian exile from here after the third Anglo-Burmese war; on the 20th of March 1945 large parts of the city were destroyed during battles between the British and Japanese unfortunately also the wood built royal palace. But numerous major sights escaped: Mandalay Hill (250 metres/820 ft. high with 1,729 steps) with temple, Kuthodaw Pagoda (729 blocks of marble inscribed with the Buddhist Tripitaka), Shwenandaw Monastery with valuable teak carvings, Mahamuni Pagoda (with rare statues of Buddha), an attractive market worth seeing (Zegyo Bazaar) with the "Diamond Jubilee Clock Tower", also recommended is a visit to the ivory carvers, gold leaf makers and weavers; and a look at the teak wharves is also rewarding. Relatively good accomodation, typical means of transport: horse drawn coaches. Excursions can be made from here to Amarapura, Sagaing, Ava and Mingun.

Mergui (F1) in Tenasserim with an island group of the same name: 400 islands around 1,000 km (620 miles) south of Rangoon famous for the pearls found and cultured there; Burma's pearls measuring 14 to 18 mm

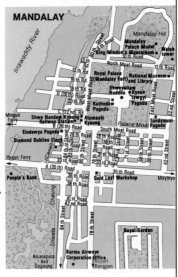

(approx. 0.5 to 0.7 inch) in diameter are considered the biggest in the world.

Mingun (*D3) attractive location 10 km from Mandalay on the east bank of the Irrawaddy, can only be reached by ferry (around 1 hour); interesting sights; the Great Bell of Mingun cast in 1790, 4 metres (13 ft.) high and weighing 87 tons, second largest in the world; Sinbyume Pagoda, Settawya Pagoda.

Mogok (*C3) 110 km (68 miles) from Mandalay; largest ruby deposits in the country and main centre for trade in jadeite. In former times the king confiscated the best stones. In 1887 the Brit-

173

ish occupied this district and took over sole rights of buying; today the mines are nationalised and the State has a monopoly on trade in precious stones.

Mon State, the some 1.3 Million Mons of the country live here mainly in the vicinity of Pegu and Moulmein; they still speak their own language but have for the most part been racially assimilated into the Birmans. The great majority of the Mon people still lives in Cambodia (Kampuchea), Vietnam and Thailand.

Moulmein (*H4) with around 150,000 inhabitants the third largest city in Burma; the River Salween opens into the Gulf of Martaban here. From 1826 to 1852 Moulmein was the main administrative town of "British Burma". Earlier famous as a port and shipbuilding town now only restricted exports of rubber, tea and rice; numerous sawmills in which working elephants are still used extensively. Sights: the Uzene Pagoda.

Mount Popa (*E2) some 50 km (31 miles) from Pagan, an andesite volcanic peak reputed to be the home of 37 Nats of Burma (see separate chapter).

Muang Tham (D4) village and temples near the village of Ban Chorake and the settlement Prakhon Chai. Is regarded as the "dream of art historians", dating back to the 10th century (completed one year later) said to be a perfect example of Khmer architecture. The 5 Prangs, main shrines, are partially ruined, beautiful stonemasonry still preserved.

Myohaung (*E1) historic town in Arakan, known earlier as Mrauk U; 80 km (50 miles) from Akyab. Very little is known of the town's origins, but it is said to have been founded in the 8th century; for more than 4 centuries capital of the Mrauk U Dynasty. Palaces, fortifications and pagodas are being swallowed more and more by the jungle.

Myitkyina (*B4) Pop. 9,000 at the foot of the Burmese spurs of the Himalays; only 50 km (31 miles) from the borders to the People's Republic of China. Close to a game park where there are said to be leopards, panther, tigers and elephants. Members of various tribes are seen in the town, mainly of the Kachin however. In January of each year there is a three day animist Manao Festival in honour of the heavenly spirits of the Kachin; today most Kachin follow Buddhism without however having surrendered their animist practices.

Nakhon Nayok (E3) 110 km (68 miles) north-east of Bangkok with two picturesque waterfalls within the neighbourhood of the town (18 km/11 miles); carnival-like atmosphere at week-ends.

Nakhon Pathom (E2) Pop. 35,000, town 55 km (34 miles) west of Bangkok, not much of interest to tourists apart from the oldest and biggest stupa in Thailand, Phra Pathom Chedi, allover height is 120 m (393′8″), without the base 115 m (377′4″); it is probable that in the 3rd/4th centuries the Mon people erected here a small stupa; in the 9th/10th centuries the Khmer set their holy tower on top; in the second half of the 19th century Rama IV had the shrine completely built over and covered in Chinese tiles. Already in 300 B.C. the Indian rajah Ashoka is said to have sent missionaries to Nakhon Pathom which at that time was almost certainly on the coast; thus this area became one of the sources of Buddhism; effigies of Buddha found show the Indian Gupta style of the 4th/5th centuries A.D. There is a museum next to the Chedi with exhibits from the Dvaravati Period.

Nakhon Phanom (B5) in the north-east province of Thailand; of strategic importance during the US-Vietnam

174

conflict; when reconnaissance troops started out from the base here; 20,000 Vietnamese refugees are said to have come here in the sixties over the Mekong.

Nakhon Ratchasima (D4) also known today as Korat. Major town of the north-east of Thailand, 265 km (164 miles) north-east of Bangkok. In addition to Thais, many Laotians live here and some Khmer; since the 13th century the town, which has nothing of real interest, was a Thai outpost which short periods of occupation by the Khmer; typical means of transport: bicycle-rickshaws. Several possibilities of good accommodation; Korat is above all important as a starting point of excursions to the Khmer temples of Phimai and Phnom Rung.

Nakhon Sawan (D2) around 300 km (186 miles) from Bangkok where the rivers Nan and Ping meet and from here form part of the Chao Phaya (Menam); no special sights but good overnight facilities.

Nakhon Si Thammarat (H2) in the south of Thailand on the Malaysian Peninsula, Pop. 60,000, some 800 km (496 miles) from Bangkok. One of the oldest Thai towns with 20 Wats built in the old town; Wat Mahatat around 30 km (18.6 miles) from the new town is one of the oldest temples in the country and the only one worth seeing here; the town is well known for exports of birds' nests to Hong Kong used in making Niello products (silver work). Relatively good accommodation available.

Ngao (A,B2) district town in the north of Thailand with elephant schools and interesting cave formations (Tham Pha Thai) close by.

Pagan (*E2) on the east bank of the Irrawaddy is, covering an area of 35 by 7 km (21.7 by 4.3 miles) the biggest concentration of pagodas in the world. There are today in this area 2.300 sacral structures (the best view is when arriving or departing by air) of which unfortunately the majority are in ruins. An earthquake on 8th July 1975 with epicentre at Pagan also destroyed many more; the extent of Pagan at the peak of its powers exceeded even that of Angkor (11th/13th centuries/Period of the Temple Builders); and is said to have had 13,000 holy structures and was named by the Chinese Mien (their name for themselves was "The City that Stamps on its Enemies"). In the "Glass Palace" chronicles of Mandalay dating from the 19th century, 55 rulers of the Pagan Dynasty are named whereby Thamudarit (107 to 152) is considered the founder; western research attributes the foundation of the Pagan Dynasty to King Anawrahta (1044 to 1077) and counts a further 10 rulers until the downfall of Pagan in 1287, whereby the son of the last ruler Narathihapati, beaten by the Mongolian hordes of Kublai Khan, Kyawswa and two rulers who followed until 1369, have not been counted; these were only puppet rulers for the Mongols or subject to the Shan realms. From Pagan Hinayana Buddhism (see separate chapter) spread throughout the land; the village which exists at the site today has some 3,000 inhabitants. The whole area is divided into the following places: Nyaung U (airport), Pagan, Myinkaba, Minnanthu, Pwasaw. In addition to sightseeing at temples and pagodas, a visit to the museum is rewarding and one to a manufacturer of lacquer work and a Burmese puppet show (next to the museum). The best hotel in all Burma is the "Thiripyitsaya" (Bungalow hotel) on the Irrawaddy and a part of the pagoda grounds, there are other (cheaper) hotels available. At least two days should be planned for sightseeing at Pagan, which is a highpoint of any visit to Burma. A show of a special kind is the sunset over the Irrawaddy, which can be watched from the Thatbyinnyu and Gawdawpalin Temples.

A list of the main, and most beautiful buildings which makes no pretence to being complete:

In Nyaung U: Kyaukgu (cave temple dating back to the 11th/12th centuries); Kyanzittha-Umin (frescoes); Shwezigon Pagoda (11th/12th centuries, prototype of Birman pagoda design); Kubyauk gyi Temple (wall painting).

In Pagan: Htilominlo Temple (large layout dating from the early 13th century); Ananda Temple (the loveliest at Pagan, 11th century); Thatbyinnyu Temple (86 metres, 12th century); Gawdawpalin Temple (60 metres, 12th/13th centuries); Bupaya Pagoda (on the banks of the Irrawaddy, 11th century, fairly small); Mahabodi Pagoda (13th century, based on Indian style of Bodh Gaya); Dhammayangyi Temple (11th century, very well preserved).

At Myinkaba: Kubyaukgyi Temple (Mon architectural style, 12th century; wall paintings); Manuha Temple (11th century; three large seated Buddhas, one giant reclining figure; built by the imprisoned Mon King Manuha of Thaton); Nanpaya Temple (right next to Manuha; is said to have been Manuha's residence; lovely reliefs on the pillars); Nagayon Temple (11th century; attractive Mon architecture); Lawkananda Pagoda (11th century, dating from the beginnings of Pagan; earlier a landmark for seafarers).

At Minnanthu: Sulamani Temple (12th century similar to Thatbyinnyu); Thambula Temple (13th century; wall paintings).

At Pwasaw: Dhammayazika Pagoda (12th century similar to Shwezigen; on terracotta panels Jatakas: scenes from the life of Buddha).

Panglong (*E4) in Shan State at which the Burmese freedom fighter Aung San concluded a treaty with representatives of ethnic minorities in which co-operation was agreed with an interim government at Rangoon on 12th February 1947; there was an agreement that several tribes could secede after 10 years membership in the Union of Burma – today a source of trouble between Rangoon and rebellious minorities.

Pasang (B2) small town 13 km (8 miles) south of Lamphun which avers it has the prettiest girls in Thailand; numerous clothing stores with cotton goods.

Pattani (A8) in the extreme south of Thailand on the Malaysian Peninsula, 1,400 km (868 miles) from Bangkok; mainly populated by Malaysian Moslems with the remains of a rajah's palace and mosque; bull and cock fighting.

Pattaya (E3) holiday resort for many European tourists on the Gulf of Thailand (140 km/87 miles from Bangkok); white, sandy, beaches, first class to good hotels, many opportunities for sports. Boat excursions to off-shore islands, lively night life.

Petchaburi (E2) around 170 km (105 miles) from Bangkok, was in earlier times the end of a caravan route from India and of major importance then; several Khmer shrines: palace of King Mongkut and the Kao Luang caves of special interest. Simple hotel accomodation.

Phangna (H1) 900 km (558 miles) distant from Bangkok, town on a gulf of the same name, which is famous for the picturesque chalk cliffs ranging out of the sea; a well known secret agent film was shot here; Than Bokkoroni National Park is close by.

Pegu (*G3) Pop. 50,000; around 90 km (56 miles) from Rangoon, a rewarding day trip (2 hours by car); Pegu founded in 573 A.D. numbers among the oldest towns in Burma and was the capital of the Mon after they were driven out of Thaton; in the 16th century capital of the united kingdom of Burma and port on the sea; captured in 1757 by the Birman King Alaungpaya and destroyed; rebuilt in 1782, from 1852 under British rule. Sigthseeing: Shwemadaw Pagoda (125 metres/410 ft., higher than Shwedagon in Rangoon, rebuilt after the war); Shwe Thalyaung Statue of the reclining Buddha (destroyed and restored several times, 60 metres (196'10") long, 17 metres (55'9") high, dating from the 10th century, rediscovered during building of the railway in 1881); Hinthagon Pagoda (name after the coat of arms of the Mon – Hinthe); Shwegugale Monastery with 64 effigies of Buddha.

Phayao (A2) provincial town in the north of Thailand; of archaeological interest as the town was built in the 11th century on the remains of an even older town; Wat Si Khom Khan with a 400 year old Buddha, 16 metres (52'6") in height, is considered the most important temple in the region.

Phitsanulok (C2) Pop. 80,000, some 500 (310 miles) from Bangkok, earlier of great significance to the Ayutthaya Dynasty because of its position. A fire in 1955 destroyed large parts of the town; worth seeing: Wat Phra Sri Ratana Mahatat with a famous bronze statue (cast in 1300) of Buddha dating from the Sukhothai Period; numerous houseboats on the Kwae Noi River and the opportunity to see displays of temple dancing. Good accommodation.

Phimai (D4) village located 56 km (35 miles) north-east of Korat with a Khmer temple complex of the same name. This is the best preserved Khmer temple outside Cambodia, erected in 1106 and 1112 by King Dharanindra-

varman I. A visit here is an absolute must on any Thailand itinerary. Close to the temple a good museum and a huge Banyan tree.

Phnom Rung (E3) famous temple of the Khmer on a mound close to the Cambodian border, south-east of Korat, still being restored. Large former ceremonial site with first class stonemasonry; you should take plenty of time for sightseeing here.

Pindaya (*E3) Buddhist cult caves with 101 statues of Buddha of varying sizes, 35 km (22 miles) from Kalaw in Shan State; wonderful panoramic view of the Shan Plateau; close to the caves a typical Shan pagoda.

Prome (*F2,3) Pop. 40,000, city in central Burma 290 km (180 miles) from Rangoon, probably founded in the 8th century by the Pyu and numbering among the oldest in the country; already mentioned in ancient Chinese chronicles; captured by Anawratha, founder of the Pagan Dynasty (1044–1077) and assimilated into the Pagan kingdom; numerous ruins can be reached by boat on the Irrawaddy, if permission is granted, or by rail; striving industrial town with important river port. Sights: Shwesandaw Pagoda with gold plated stupa.

Rangoon (*G,H3) capital of Burma (see separate chapter). Sightseeing: Shwe Dagon Pagoda; Sule Pagodel Botataung Pagoda; harbour on Rangoon River; National Museum; Market; Zoo; Diplomatic Quarter. No night life. Burmese dance at the Karaweik Restaurant highly recommended. Mingaladon Airport around 20 km outside the city. Strong evidence of British influence at the city centre, several relatively good hotels (the best: Inya Lake followed by the Strand Hotel). Political and financial centre of the country, still limping behind Mandalay as far as cultural life is concerned.

Rat Buri(E2) 120 km (75 miles) southwest of Bangkok; today 30 km (19 miles) from the Gulf of Siam, in the past direct on the sea; Wat Mahatat with murals of the Ayutthaya Period, very rare; 10 km (6 miles) away Dvaravati period temples (10th century) at Kubua.

Rayong (E3) 220 km (137 miles) from Bangkok on the Gulf; famed for its fish sauce "Nam pla", which is part of every Thai meal.

Rose Garden (E3) recreational park with hotels, restaurants, golf course some 30 km (19 miles) from Bangkok; mainly built with tourists in mind, entertainment centre with traditional dance and shows: daily at 3 p.m. the so-called "Thai Village Show" takes place plus demonstrations of Thai handicrafts.

Sagaing (*D3) for the first time in 1315 capital of the Shan princes; 15 km (9 miles) from Mandalay (around 45 minutes by car) with a crossing of the Ava (Sagaing) Bridge; chain of hills with monasteries and pagodas of impressive architecture. Especially worth seeing: Kaung Hmu Daw Pagoda built in Ceylonese style; Sun U Ponya Shin Pagoda (draws many visitors, best panoramic view over the hills with around 600 sacral sites); U Min Kyauksee Pagoda; some 5,000 monks live at Sagaing today and the site is still a centre of Buddhism.

Sandoway (*F2) Burmese bathing resort on the Bay of Bengal with a Beach Hotel; recently foreigners have been admitted here, it can be reached via daily flights from Rangoon; lovely beaches of fine white sand, the favourite located close to the fishing village of Ngapali; in the 1st century A.D. Sandoway was the main port en-route between India and the Indonesian islands, the city was at the time called Dvaravati; Buddha is said to have spent three of the 547 lives described in the Jatakas here. Pagodas: Nandaw, Sandaw and Andaw.

San Kamphaeng. (B2) 14 km (9 miles) from Chiangmai, village of silk spinners, with opportunity for shopping.

Sara Buri (D3) located around 130 km (81 miles) from Bangkok without any really spectacular sights; close to the town is the well known Mondhop of the Wat Phra Buddha Badh; splendid holy shrine with fantastic decorative work over Buddha's footprint.

Sattahip (E3) on the east coast of Thailand, 170 km (106 miles) from Bangkok; Thai Royal Navy support point, formerly base of the US Navy. Only trip of any interest: a drive in the morning to the fishing village to watch the boats coming in with their catch.

Si Satchanalai (B,C2) the ancient Sawankhalok some 500 km (310 miles) north of Bangkok on the River Yom; an early Mon settlement which became the sister city of the old Sukhothai; flourished in the 13th/14th centuries; also known for the manufacture of celadon which was introduced by Ram Kamheng who brought Chinese porcelain specialists back with him from his visit to Beijing, who then settled near Sawankhalok; many ancient firing ovens have been found; worth visiting: Wat Phra Prang (Wat Mahathai) with Buddha in Sukhothai style; Wat Chedi Chet Theo with the remains of frescoes; Wat Chang Lom showing Ceylonese influence.

Songkla (A7) 1,320 km (820 miles) from Bangkok is reputed to be the most attractive beach resort on the Gulf of Thailand; pretty fishing villages, coconut and rubber plantations. Wat Klang with beautiful wall paintings

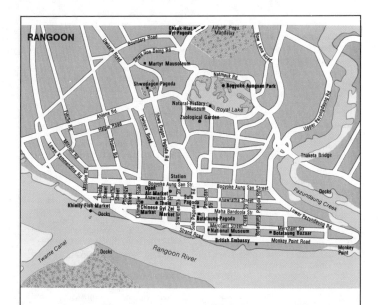

RANGOON

from the era of King Rama IV. Relatively good accommodation.

Sri Ksetra (*F2,3) ruined city right next to Prome; capital of the first known Pyu realms with preserved temples and pagodas in brick (5th to 8th century). Payama Pagoda; Paya Gyi Pagoda; Bawpawgyi Pagoda; Yahandargu Temple.

Sukhothai (C2) "Cradle of Thai Culture" 460 km (286 miles) north of Bangkok; the first great Thai kingdom was founded here on the soil of Thailand (see separate chapter); the direction followed here influenced the art traditions throughout the country; in addition to numerous religious structures, the museum, with many first class exhibits, is also worth visiting. Major sights: Wat Mahathat (King's

Temple, which served as the prototype for Wat Phra Keo in Bangkok); Wat Si Chum (Buddha 14 metres/46 ft high; climbing up to the roof on the 3 metre/ 9'10" wide wall has recently been banned); Wat Sra Sri with a mighty Buddha in Ceylonese style before the Chedi; Wat Chetupon (Vihan with two statues of Buddha). Delicacy in Sukhothai of today: pate made of roasted, ground, beetles.

Surat Thani (H2) on the Malayan Peninsula around 670 km (416 miles) from Bangkok; busy commercial and shipping town. Ferries go from here to Ko Samui.

Surin (D5) 670 km (416 miles) northeast of Bangkok, town of the silk spinners, without any really interesting sights; once a year Surin comes to life;

80 to 100 elephants take part in the Elephant round-up in November (see separate chapter).

Syriam (*H3) 20 km (12.5 miles) from Rangoon possible as a day trip by ferry on the River Rangoon. Pop. 20,000. In this Portuguese style town, the seafarer de Brito fought his way, from 1600 for 13 years, to the throne of Syriam (see separate chapter); remains of Portuguese baroque buildings, the "floating pagoda" Kyauktan and the lovely Kyauk Khauk Pagoda.

Tagaung (*C3) 200 km (124 miles) from Mandalay in a northerly direction on the Irrawaddy; is considered the cradle of Burmese culture; according to legends the town was founded some years before Buddha's birth, and then built for a second time around 600 B.C. And it is said that plans for founding Sri Ksetra initiated here. The city is mentioned for the first time in an inscription in Pagan dating from the 12th century and it is believed that at the time Tagaung was called Old Pagan and flourished during the same era. Excavations have also confirmed early connections between Tagaung and Sri Ksetra. Today only the semi-ruined Shwezigon Pagoda can be seen.

Tak (C2) some 510 km (317 miles) north of Bangkok, earlier a flourishing port on the Ping for trading between Bangkok and Chiang Mai; a colourful market is still in existence and excursions are possible to the Bhumipol Dam.

Taunggyi (*E4) main administrative centre of the Shan, can be reached from Heho after arrival by air. Formerly a popular "hill station" among the British colonialists because of the pleasant climate; starting point for trips on the Inle Lake; good hotel available. A visit to the small museum, with costumes of the ethnic minorities on show, is re-

warding as is the lively market offering a large variety of wares. The so-called night market is where trading takes place in goods smuggled from Thailand. From Taunggyi the road goes through the area dominated by rebel tribes to Kengtun, capital of the Golden Triangle.

Taungu (*F3) also known as Toungoo, around 300 km (186 miles) north of Rangoon on the River Sittang; the political demarcation line between Upper and Lower Burma runs through here; Taungu was the source of the second great Burmese empire (see separate chapter).

Tavoy (E1) town north of the Mergui Archipelago on the coast of Tenasserim with nice beaches; the Inthas of Inle Lake, today famous as leg rudders, came from this area originally.

Tha Ton (A2) 25 km (15.5 miles) from Fang and located close to the Burmese border which is the starting point for a really adventurous trip by river to Chiang Rai (not recommended at present for security reasons).

Thaton (*H4) ancient capital of the Mon, north of Moulmein, which was conquered by the Pagan King Anawrahta (see separate chapter).

Thon Buri (E3) sister city of Bangkok on the west bank of the Chao Phaya (Menam); founded after the fall of the Ayutthaya Dynasty by General Taksin prior to Bangkok's becoming, a little later, the capital in 1782. Three bridges connect Thon Buri, Pop. 500,000, with Bangkok, 2 large canals and several small Khlongs complete the transport network; there are of course ferries. Thon Buri is for all practical purposes today a part of the capital, worth seeing is Wat Arun which should be included in every sightseeing tour.

Timland (E3) 20 km (12.5 miles) north of Bangkok and erected as a recreational centre, similar to the Rose Garden (see under this name).

Trat (F4) 400 km (250 miles) from Bangkok and chief town of the province of the same name on the border to Cambodia; completely unspoiled natural countryside with few tourist facilities.

Ubon Ratchathani (D6) town located on the banks of the Mun 680 km (423 miles) from Bangkok, very lively. The full translation of the name means "Royal City of the Lotus Blossom". One of the best preserved Wats of North Thailand is found here. During the sixties a US air base.

Udon Thani (B4) formerly a wayside stop on the road to Laos, 560 km (348 miles) north-east of Bangkok with 80,000 inhabitants. Bars, night clubs and hotels all date from the time Udon was an American air base; weird sandstone formations in the vicinity.

Yasothon (C5) 820 km (510 miles) north-east of Bangkok is only really interesting once a year: before the start of the monsoon in May metre high colourfully decorated rockets are set off which are home made; these are intended as requests for rain and good harvests.

Yaunghwe (*E4) at the north end of the Inle Lake, the biggest village here. Boat trips across the lake start here, simple accommodation for those who don't want to live in Taunggyi.

Thailand

Currency in circulation:

Notes	Baht	1, 5, 10, 20, 100, 500
Coins	Satang	1, 5, 10, 25, 50
	Baht	1, 5, 10, 20, 50, 100, 150

Burma

Currency in circulation:

Notes:

Rupee	1, 5, 10
Kyat	1, 5, 10, 20, 50, 100

Coins:

Pyas	1, 5, 10, 25, 50, 1 Kyat
Rupee	¼, ½.

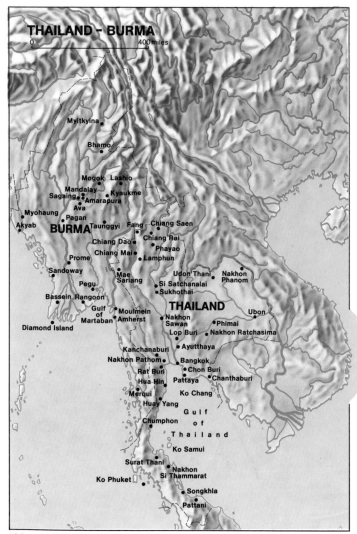

THAILAND - BURMA

0 _____ 400miles

Myitkyina

Bhamo

Mogok Lashio
Mandalay
Sagaing Kyaukme
Amarapura
Ava
Myohaung Pagan
Akyab BURMA Taunggyi Fang Chiang Saen
Chiang Dao Chiang Rai
Chiang Mai Phayao
Prome Lamphun
Sandoway Mae Udon Thani Nakhon
Pegu Sariang Si Satchanalai Phanom
Bassein Rangoon Sukhothai
Gulf Moulmein THAILAND Ubon
of Amherst Nakhon
Martaban Sawan Phimai
Diamond Island Lop Buri Nakhon Ratchasima
Kanchanaburi Ayutthaya
Nakhon Pathom Bangkok
Rat Buri Chon Buri
Hua Hin Pattaya Chanthaburi
Merqui Ko Chang
Huay Yang
Chumphon G u l f
o f
T h a i l a n d
Ko Samui
Surat Thani Nakhon
Ko Phuket Si Thammarat
Songkhla
Pattani

Useful Information

Passports, Visas
As a general rule a valid passport in conjunction with a transit or return ticket for stays up to 15 days. For stays up to 60 days a visa is normally required. Regulations applicable to citizens of your own country can be obtained from Thai embassies, consulates, etc.

In as far as Burma is concerned, a valid passport with at least two unused pages in conjunction with a transit or return ticket, plus a visa for a stay of 7 days. Stays of more than 7 days are only possible in exceptional cases upon special application.

Burma can be reached by sea or air, but not overland; since however as a general rule shipping services from Burma don't run in a way which ensures keeping to the 7 day restriction, these can be forgotten for all practical purposes. The best route by air is from Bangkok and all flights go without exception to Rangoon, which means that any round trips have to start from here. Visas are best obtained previously in your own country they can however be obtained in Bangkok (handled quickly at Diethelm Travel, 544 Ploenchit Road, Tel.: 2 52 40 41-9 and Arlymea Travel Co., 113/5 Suriwong Road, Tel.: 23 4 93 31-3).

Vaccinations
Vaccinations are not stipulated for Thailand, but a cholera vaccination is required in Burma: these have to be entered into the International Vaccination Certificate. Steps against malaria are also recommended.

Travel Insurance
Also recommended is travel insurance for baggage/accident/third party/and health (a so-called package deal).

First Aid
Whilst most western medicines and remedies are available in Bangkok, supplies are not assured in Burma. For this reason any personal medication should be included in baggage, in adequate supplies, plus a remedy against stomach and intestinal upsets, colds, headaches and a multi-vitamin preparation and adhesive plasters (or spray type wound dressing).

Clothing
Light cotton or linen clothing, headgear against the sun, bathing suits, light but strong, shoes, rainwear. Evening, cocktail, dress is only really expected in the big luxury hotels in Bangkok, and even here clothing can at times be casual (men for instance don't have to wear ties).

Shorts are frowned on at the temples in Thailand and Burma, as well as all too revealing clothing. Temple visitors are expected to go barefoot without exception, which means that sandals are useful (easily slipped off). When visiting the Royal Palace in Bangkok shorts are absolutely forbidden and men have to roll down shirt sleeves. Any hats etc., have to be removed. Semi-nude (topless) bathing is strictly forbidden in Burma and not exactly welcome in Thailand (always bear in mind the almost puritanical attitude of Thais and Burmese towards sex in public).

A warm sweater or light jacket is needed in the North of Thailand and Shan State in Burma, in the evenings.

Money, Currency

Currency in **Thailand** is the Baht and each Baht equals 100 Satang. As from Nov. '84 rates are no longer based on the US$. Ask your bank for current rates.

Currency in **Burma** is the Kyat, each Kyat equals 100 Pya. For current exchange rates please ask your bank.

Burmese currency may not be taken into or out of the country. In Thailand, the limit for local currency is 2,000 bath; there is no limit on foreign currency. Cash and traveller's cheques have to be declared. The currency declaration has to be submitted when changing Baht or Kyat back into another currency. The amount of foreign currency taken out of both countries may not, under any circumstances, be more than that brought in.

In Burma the currency declaration has to be handed over every time money is changed, and authorized exchange offices (banks) enter the amounts involved. Make sure this declaration is kept in a safe place.

Money can be changed in the main terminals at both Bangkok and Rangoon airports. There are porters for baggage available (5 Baht/2 Kyat per bag), there are tourist information offices at both airports.

Arrival, Customs

Entry into Thailand is completely unproblematic: 200 cigarettes, 250 gr. tobacco and 1 litre spirits duty free; there is a ban on import of fire-arms, narcotics, pornography and goods apparently for trading. Antiques may only be taken out when a certificate is issued by the "Fine Arts Department" (in Bangkok: Na Phrathat Road, Tel.: 2 21 48 17). Buddha statues old or otherwise, may not be taken out, and there is a ban on export of old pottery from Bang Chiang.

Entry into Burma at Rangoon Airport (Mingaladon) is somewhat more of a problem; baggage checks are thorough and there is a time consuming customs declaration to be completed listing all personal belongings such as cameras, electronic equipment, tape or cassette recorders, watches, jewellery, etc. When leaving the country again this declaration has to be submitted together with the currency declaration. Duty free are 200 cigarettes, or 50 cigars or 8 ounces tobacco, 1 litre spirits, a half litre Eau de Cologne or perfume. Import of fire-arms, pornography, anything in writing directed against the state, narcotics, is forbidden.

Antiques and precious stones not bought at the "Diplomatic Store" or other state owned store, may not be exported.

Transportation

Taxis into town from both airports, which lie outside the towns. Short stays in Bangkok can be spent at the new "Airport Hotel", numerous hotels in Bangkok offer free transportation from the airport to hotel.

Tourist Information
In Thailand:

Tourist Authority of Thailand, Ratchadamnoen Nok Avenue, <u>Bangkok</u>, Tel.: 28 21 14 37
Branch offices:
<u>Dom Muang Airport</u>,
Tel.: 5 23 89 72 – 3,
<u>Chiang Mai</u>: 135 Praisani Road, Tel.: 23 53 34,
<u>Pattaya</u>: Chaihat Road, Tel.: 41 87 50
<u>Phuket</u>: 73–75 Phuket Road, Tel.: 21 22 13

In Burma:

Tourist Burma,
77–79 Sule Pagoda Road, <u>Rangoon</u>
(visit in person recommended)

Branch offices:
Mingaladon Airport.
There are other offices in Mandalay, Pagan and Taunggyi (contact made via the hotels there).

In Thailand several up-to-date magazines give information on the latest events, these are obtainable at hotels free of charge.

Business hours
Thailand:
Banks: Monday to Friday 8.30 a.m. to 3.30 p.m.
Government Offices: Monday to Friday 8.30 a.m. to 4.30 p.m.
Shops and Stores: there are no official hours of opening, most are opened throughout from 9 a.m. to 6 p.m. and some shops close later.
Post Office: Monday to Friday 8 a.m. to 6 p.m.
Saturday, Sunday and Holidays from 9 a.m. to 1 p.m.

Burma:
Banks: Monday to Friday 10 a.m. to 2 p.m.
Saturday: 10 a.m. to 12 noon.
Government Offices: Monday to Friday 9.30 a.m. to 4 p.m.
Saturday 9 a.m. to 12 noon.
Shops and Stores: no fixed hours.
Post Office: Monday to Saturday 8 a.m. to 9 p.m.
Sundays and holidays 8 a.m. to 8 p.m.

Voltage
220 V in both countries, any adapters needed should be brought from home.

Health Care
A few basic rules which apply to both countries:
– Never drink unboiled water, even in the best hotels.
– Use bottled water for cleaning your teeth.

– Don't eat ice cream (except in good hotels in Bangkok).
– Don't drink ice cold drinks during the day.
– Don't eat unpeeled fruits.
– Don't eat unpeeled vegetables (salads!).
– Take care with air conditioning (risk of colds and chills).
– Protect yourself against the sun.
– Take a sweater or jacket for cool evenings (North Thailand/Shan State).

Medical Care
Available in Thailand in most places, even in the provinces. Only assured in Burma at the main tourist areas.

Photography
No difficulty in either country, except inside temples and museums where photography is not allowed. When taking pictures of anyone, politeness always pays and asking for permission doesn't hurt either. Film can be bought in all towns of any size in Thailand, for Burma on the other hand you should take enough film with you since here it is not always obtainable and often old.

Laundry
There is an express service at most larger hotels in Thailand (washing comes back on the same day). For Burma it's advisable to take enough with you since stays are too short at most places to guarantee getting laundry back in time.

Admission Charges
are payable at temples and museums in both countries, but are relatively cheap throughout.

Guides
Can be hired in both countries, in Thailand however it's recommended that only authorized guides are used. In Burma the guide from "Tourist Burma"

is either available from Rangoon for the whole trip, or at each place visited (Pagan, Mandalay, charges are reasonable).

Tipping
Tips for personal services are expected all over: Some tourists have a reputation for being a bit miserly in this respect, don't be too careful with tips, these are a part of what are anyway very low wages for those employed in any way in the tourist trade. The roomboy at the hotel for instance around 20 to 25 US cents per night minimum; porters at least 5 Baht or 2 Kyat each bag; services in restaurants not under 10 Baht. In Burma, offered discreetly, since tipping is officially frowned on, 4 Kyat.

Registration
Foreigners in Burma have to register at the local police station wherever they stay. If you are at a tourist hotel, this will be taken care of for you.

Round Trips
Burma is almost certainly one of the most attractive travel destinations on earth, the only drawback being that the restriction to stays of 7 days narrows down the opportunities for round trips. For this reason many tour operators have combined the highpoints of Lower and Upper Burma in air tours which leave enough time to see and enjoy the major sights.
1st Day: Arrival in Rangoon from Bangkok. Evening the first trip to Shwe Dagon Pagoda by taxi.
2nd Day: Morning flight Rangoon – Heho; then on to Taunggyi with museum and market.
3rd Day: Trip to Inle Lake in the morning; several hours boat trip from Yaunghwe to Phaung Daw with "floating market". Return to Heho and flight to Mandalay.

4th Day: Sightseeing in Mandalay.
5th Day: Morning flight to Pagan, first sightseeing excursion.
6th Day: Sightseeing in Pagan and afternoon return flight to Rangoon.
7th Day: Morning, sightseeing in Rangoon (Sule and Botataung Pagodas, market, harbour and Shwe Dagon Pagoda); afternoon departure for Bangkok.

For those who can't make this round trip then a half day excursion to Pegu or Syriam is recommended; those more thirsty for adventure can, with special permission, make the 3 day excursion from Rangoon to Kyaik-tiyo (gilded cliffs); hiking to the cliffs crowned by the small pagoda takes six hours in both directions. The only accommodation offered here is at the monastery inn (1st day: Rangoon – Kyaik-tiyo; 2nd day: hiking; 3rd day: return to Rangoon). Anyone wishing to enjoy the Burmese beaches can take the flight excursion to Sandoway (at least 3 days are needed) on the Gulf of Bengal (also subject to special permission).

A stay of 14 days is possible in Thailand without a visa, and tourists have enough time to visit the most interesting places. There are so many round trips on offer that the list which follows can in no way be taken as being complete, it is only intended to give an indication of what can be undertaken.

Grand Tour of Thailand
1st Day: Bangkok
2nd Day: Bangkok – Bang Pa-in – Ayutthaya – Korat
3rd Day: Excursion to Khmer Temples, Phnom Rung and Phimai
4th Day: Korat – Saraburi – Lopburi
5th Day: Lopburi – Phitsanulok
6th Day: Phitsanulok – Lampang (with Sukhothai)
7th Day: Lampang – Phayao – Chiang Rai

8th Day: Excursion to mountain tribes and Chiangsaen on the border to Laos
9th Day: Boat trip on the River Kok, Chiang Rai – Chiang Mai
10th Day: Chiang Mai
11th Day: Return flight to Bangkok
12th Day: Trip to Pattaya
13th Day: Pattaya
14th Day: Return to Bangkok, and homeward bound.

The emphasis is on cultural sights in this Grand Tour, tourists looking for more leisure and relaxation can leave out the east of Thailand and travel by the most direct route to Saraburi and Lopburi. This means an extra two days at the beaches. Also recommended is the 2 day excursion from Bangkok to the River Kwai with overnight stay at the romantic lodge there (Bangkok – Kanchanapuri – River Kwai – Boat Trip, trip on the "Death Railroad" – return to Bangkok).

In addition to Pattaya, Cha-am is becoming more and more popular as a beach resort; and Hua Hin and Phuket can also be recommended.
At least 2, and even better 3, days should be planned for sight-seeing and shopping in Bangkok.

Please note: it is not always safe to travel alone in the North, West and South of Thailand, especially after dark.

Contents

Hildebrand's Travel Guides

Hildebrand's Travel Maps

1. Balearic Islands Majorca 1:185,000, Minorca, Ibiza, Formentera 1:125,000
2. Tenerife 1:100,000, La Palma, Gomera, Hierro 1:190,000
3. Canary Islands Gran Canaria 1:100,000, Fuerteventura, Lanzarote 1:190,000
4. Spanish Coast I Costa Brava, Costa Blanca 1:900,000, General Map 1:2,500,000
5. Spanish Coast II Costa del Sol, Costa de la Luz 1:900,000, General Map 1:2,500,000
6. Algarve 1:100,000, Costa do Estoril 1:400,000
7. Gulf of Naples 1:200,000, Ischia 1:35,000, Capri 1:28,000
8. Sardinia 1:200,000
*9. Sicily 1:200,000 Lipari (Aeolian) Islands 1:30,000
11. Yugoslavian Coast I Istria – Dalmatia 1:400,000 General Map 1:2,000,000
12. Yugoslavian Coast II Southern Dalmatia – Montenegro 1:400,000 General Map 1:2,000,000
13. Crete 1:200,000
15. Corsica 1:200,000
16. Cyprus 1:350,000
17. Israel 1:360,000
18. Egypt 1:1,500,000
19. Tunisia 1:900,000

20. Morocco 1:900,000
21. New Zealand 1:2,000,000
22. Sri Lanka (Ceylon), Maldive Islands 1:750,000
23. Jamaica 1:400,000
24. USA, Southern Canada 1:3,500,000
25. India 1:4,255,000
26. Thailand, Burma, Malaysia 1:2,800,000, Singapore 1:139,000
27. Western Indonesia 1:12,700,000, Sumatra 1:3,570,000, Java 1:1,887,000, Bali 1:597,000, Celebes 1:3,226,000
28. Hong Kong 1:116,000, Macao 1:36,000
29. Taiwan 1:700,000
30. Philippines 1:2,860,000
31. Australia 1:5,315,000
32. South Africa 1:3,360,000
33. Seychelles General Map 1:6,000,000, Mahé 1:96,000, Praslin 1:65,000, La Digue 1:52,000, Silhouette 1:84,000, Frégate 1:25,000
34. Hispaniola (Haiti, Dominican Republic) 1:816,000
35. Soviet Union General Map 1:15,700,000, Western Soviet Union 1:9,750,000, Black Sea Coast 1:3,500,000

*37. Madeira
38. Mauritius 1:125,000
39. Malta 1:38,000
40. Majorca 1:125,000, Cabrera 1:75,000
41. Turkey 1:1,655,000
42. Cuba 1:1,100,000
43. Mexico 1:3,000,000
44. Korea 1:800,000
45. Japan 1:1,600,000
46. China 1:5,400,000
47. USA: The West 1:3,500,000
48. USA: The East 1:3,500,000
49. East Africa 1:2,700,000
50. Greece: Southern Mainland, Peloponnese 1:400,000
51. Central Europe 1:2,000,000
52. Portugal 1:500,000
53. Puerto Rico, Virgin Islands, St. Croix 1:294,000
54. The Caribbean Guadeloupe 1:165,000 Martinique 1:125,000 St. Lucia 1:180,000 St. Martin 1:105,000 Barthélemy 1:60,000 Dominica 1:175,000 General Map 1:5,000,000
55. Réunion 1:127,000
56. Czechoslovakia 1:700,000
57. Hungary 1:600,000

*in print